T · H · E
JUDDS

T·H·E

JUDDS

A Biography

by

BOB MILLARD

A DOLPHIN BOOK
Doubleday
NEW YORK   LONDON   TORONTO   SIDNEY

Dolphin and the portrayal of two dolphins
are trademarks of Doubleday, a division of
Bantam Doubleday Dell Publishing Group, Inc.

Library of Congress Cataloging-in-Publication Data
Millard, Bob, 1951–
The Judds: a biography / by Bob Millard.
p. cm.
"A Dolphin book."
1. Judds (Musical group) 2. Country musicians—United States—
Biography. I. Title.
ML421.J82M5 1988
784.5'2'00922—dc19

[B]   87-37952
CIP
MN

BG

Acknowledgments

I am indebted to many people for their help and contributions to this book. Among the community of writers whose livelihood derives, at least in part, from covering entertainers and the entertainment industry, there are some real pros who coincidentally happen to be very generous human beings. That they shared their own primary source materials, contacts, rumors, gossip, tips, deliciously (and often appropriately) cynical senses of humor, plus their professional time and talents was a great source of encouragement and satisfaction for me. They are good friends, old and new, from the fraternity of persons whose job it is to suffer the egos and sift through the hype of the entertainment industry in order to produce objective and accurate stories on deadline.

The following writers have my most sincere and heartfelt thanks for their substantial contributions of material, time, and ideas: Bob Allen, Ellie Brecker, Patrick Carr, Diane Comer, Ed Morris, Alanna Nash, and Robert K. Oermann. They gave me their best. Any errors found within these pages are my own.

Some material in this book originally appeared in, and is reprinted by permission of, *Country Music* magazine, *Country Song Roundup, Music City News,* and the *Gavin Report.*

From each of these publications, respectively, I especially wish to thank Russell Barnard, Rick Bolsom, Neil Pond, and Lisa Smith for their cooperation. Thanks are also due to the Country Music Foundation Library and its staff, as well as to Ellen Wood, Melodye Busbin, and Betsy Bateman of BMI and Tom Long of ASCAP, for their help in researching and making contact with their affiliated songwriters.

I especially wish to thank all the sources quoted in these pages from my own interviews. Their perspectives and insights contributed to making this biography a more interesting and substantial story than it might otherwise have been. Some I quoted, and others I did not. All are sincerely appreciated. Their recollections filled in a lot of gaps in my research and provided unique first-hand accounts of the lives and career development of two unique persons: Naomi and Wynonna Judd.

There are so many others who helped me with information, anecdotes, or just encouragement, and I thank them all. For providing his country home as the perfect retreat for late-inning writing, I am much obliged to Ashley Wiltshire. For constant patience and encouragement, my wife Lucinda Smith has all my love and deepest appreciation. I also wish to thank Madeleine Morel of 2M Communications and Casey Fuetsch of Doubleday/Dolphin Books for their continued efforts and faith in me. It also behooves me to thank Naomi and Wynonna Judd for having, as it turned out, lives that were even more interesting than their publicity.

BOB MILLARD

Contents

Contents

O·N·E

Growing Up in Ashland, Kentucky

The delivery room of King's Daughters' Hospital was only a couple of blocks from the house in downtown Ashland, Kentucky, where Charles Glen Judd and Pauline Ruth Oliver Judd lived. Glen and Polly got a several months' head start on the official post–World War II baby boom when daughter Diana Ellen Judd was born there January 11, 1946. The baby's middle name came from her grandmother Ellen Judd. Years later, when she discarded Diana for the more colorful appellation Naomi, she would keep her middle name for sentimental reasons.

Ashland in 1946 was a bustling river town with ten thousand people. Split between Boyd and Greenup counties in the westernmost part of the Appalachian Mountains, Ashland is high up in the northeastern part of Kentucky. It sits close to the ground on the banks of the Ohio River just across from Coal Grove, Ohio, a ragged rural community edging out from the barge ports for cement, sand, and coal tipples that line that side of the riverbank. A few miles south is the border with West Virginia. Young people on both sides of the

Ohio River cross over the bridge that runs into Winchester Street, to flash fake IDs and buy booze in each other's states. Young Ohio and West Virginia couples in a hurry know well the speed with which they can accomplish an elopement in Catlettsburg, outside of Ashland.

The Ashland Oil Company was headquartered in the town when Diana was growing up. It owned and operated producing wells, crude oil pipelines, a fleet of river barges for hauling both crude and refined products, and the tall "cat crackers" that distilled gasoline and naphtha out of crude oil. You couldn't miss the refinery smell—the smell of progress some said—when the winds were right. Its retail products included Valvoline motor oils and Ashland motor fuels, sold through a regional chain of service stations. Ashland Oil was one of the top employers in the city and one of the most important industrial names on the civic map. By the early 1950s, in the center of the town which gave its name to one of its largest industries, you could find Glen Judd's Ashland Station—the biggest in the city, the pride of its operator and the bread and butter of his growing family.

Glen Judd's business thrived, for if ever there was a golden age of the automobile in America, it was the 1950s. Auto manufacturers had learned how to crank out tanks, jeeps, and troop-carrying trucks at high speed during the recent war. They perfected the basic process once their Detroit assembly lines were released back to peacetime production. De Sotos, Packards, Hudsons, Lincolns, Fords, and Chevrolets were rolling off the car lots and onto the roads, where they would need gasoline, lubricants, and eventually, service work. It was a boom time all over the nation, a good time to be alive and an especially good time to be anywhere in the automobile sales or service business. Glen and Polly's family grew right along with the service station. Soon Diana Ellen had as siblings Brian, Margaret, and Mark.

Far from having had a childhood of rural poverty, Diana Ellen Judd grew up in a comfortable middle-class home, which her family bought outright from her grandparents when she was about four years old. Located on the twenty-two-hundred block of Montgomery Avenue, the house is in a neighborhood of substantial residential buildings, large town homes on small lots, many in the immediate area having the renovated elegance of a historic district. A couple of blocks away were the Paramount and Capital theaters, where Diana and friends from Crabbe Elementary School walked to watch movies on Saturday afternoons. Nearby are the well-kept playgrounds, ball fields, and expansive green space offered by Ashland's Central Park.

"I had a very happy childhood in Ashland," Naomi said. "My dad owned a filling station, where he was in business for himself. We lived in a big house, and I could walk to everything I needed, including all three schools I went to."

Diana's mother was a housewife and the superintendent of the nursery at the First Baptist Church. She sheltered her children as much as possible from the hardships of life around them. Her own childhood had been shattered at age twelve, when her father got up from the dining-room table, walked into the back room, put a gun to his head, and bought heaven with a pull of the trigger. Polly's religion was very real to her, as was her desire to give her own children stability and a strict Christian upbringing that equated cleanliness with godliness. She and her husband considered their very tidy hearth and home the center of their universe and seldom left for long without taking the children with them. Their big getaway was to drive down the Atlantic coast to Myrtle Beach, South Carolina.

"I was raised in a wonderful small town atmosphere," Naomi recalled. "I can only remember three afternoons that [my mom] was not there when I came home from school, waiting with a snack and asking 'What did you do today, honey.' "

A favorite weekend retreat for the Judd children was the farmhouse of their grandparents Roy Ogden and Ellen Judd on a feeder stream of the Ohio known locally as Little Cat Creek, near Louisa, Kentucky. Naomi still wistfully recalls evenings on Little Cat Creek, where nature serenaded with the lush countryside symphony of crickets and whippoor-wills.

"When I was a little girl I'd go visit my grandparents out in the country," she said. "I'd go out in the woods by myself, and I was like a wild animal: unlimited imagination. I'd come home filthy dirty, with black rings around my arms, like a child of the wolves or something."

Diana was a child who loved to daydream and fantasize. Make-believe was her favorite game, and she sometimes lost herself in the worlds she created in her imagination. One of her favorite fantasies was that she was an Indian princess. It was a compelling and exotic fantasy for her. Sometimes the games were so powerfully real in her mind that she wondered whether she might really be the misplaced child of some Cherokee or Chippewa royalty. There was, after all, the hint of Indian blood somewhere in her ancestry. On those occasions she would make up mellifluous Indian-sounding names for herself.

Diana's country relatives, mostly on her father's side of the family, had innumerable pieces of rural lore to teach her —things she would treasure as her heritage. Her Aunt Zora ran a little shotgun-style one-room country store, and she taught Diana how to identify snakes. Her grandfather Judd taught her enough to be able to let her run free in the deep woods on his farm.

"When I was a little kid my mama and daddy would take us kids out to my grandpa Judd's farm every weekend, and we spent summers out there," she said. "Granddaddy . . . taught me, that when I went out in the woods to play, how to tell time. I'd look at the bottom of the sunset, and however many fingers I could get in between the bottom of the sunset and the top of the highest ridge was fifteen minutes apiece for each finger. That's how I knew how long I had before the sun went down."

As a child, she roamed the woods and pastures of that farm and those of other Judd kinfolk, playing games and roles that she made up as she went along.

Diana certainly didn't get her penchant for freewheeling, dramatic fantasy from her mother. Polly Judd is a private and unassuming woman to the general public, but to her children she was strict and stoic, hiding her emotions so well that when tragedy struck the family years later her release of them shocked Diana greatly. Polly wanted to make sure that her children were inculcated with those values and beliefs that she herself held most dear. Tenacious and demanding, she passed on to her first born not only her basic values but her stubbornness as well.

Polly Judd mixed her faith in the Lord's palpable omniscience with the prevailing hygienic prophylaxis against poliomyelitis, or infantile paralysis, as it was popularly known. Polio, thought in folklore to be spread in part by house flies, was a great crippler and killer of children and young adults as late as the mid-1950s. President Franklin Roosevelt had his legs paralyzed by it in his youth. In adulthood Naomi would recall vividly her mother's Sunday school admonition that "Jesus and germs are everywhere, girls, so always say your prayers and wash your hands." Diana internalized the stirring emotions of this religion, correspondingly developing a compulsion for neatness. Her fetish for cleanliness would extend into an overt hostility toward disease, taking illness as a personal challenge, almost an insult.

Diana was a bright, beautiful, and physically active child, friendly and well-known among her peers. Softball and swimming were two of her favorite sports, and she developed a spontaneous and whimsical sense of humor. She was a good student and showed some early musical talent, but there was no indication during her formative years that singing would ever be an important part of her life. Her mother even jokingly accused her of having "lip-synced the hymns in church."

"She was a good pianist," Diana's mother told the Ashland *Daily Independent.* "She studied with Elizabeth Johnson here. I had thought at the time that with her dramatic ability and outgoing determination, she might become an actress, but I didn't think of her ever going into country music. She hadn't expressed a desire to sing as a child."

But Diana seemed to lack a sense of control in her life. Her parents exercised complete authority, leaving perhaps too little room for the child to develop a sense of herself as an effective individual. She became secretly shy. Her early feelings of self-esteem often came in the biggest doses in her fantasies of importance and mystery. It wasn't only Diana's make-believe games that told her mother that the child might have acting in her future. Diana was very dramatic in presenting her case when she wanted something or in expressing her opinions. Even her childhood friends noticed her tendency to carry drama to far lengths.

Russell Powell, now the editor of the Ashland *Daily Independent,* has been a friend of Diana's since they were in grammar school together. He remembered a particular event that illuminates her off-the-wall sense of humor and her possession of a special gift for role playing as early as fourteen years old.

"I remember when we were all in the eighth grade," Powell recalled one afternoon in his office. "A girl around the corner from the Judds' house gave a costume party. One girl came dressed in a leopard-skin leotard with a long wig that fell over the front of her face so we couldn't see who it was. She had a rock in each hand like a cave man, or Alley Oop, and she came in and sat in the corner and pounded those rocks together for the longest time. She kept her face down so we really couldn't tell who it was. Finally, she got up and said something to someone and really surprised us all because it was Diana.

"You know, most kids who would do something like that, they might keep it up for a few minutes before they would yell 'Hey, it's me, didn't I fool you?' But Diana just went on and on with it."

At twelve, she finished Coles Junior High and started in at Ashland High School. She found out that hers would be the first class that wouldn't graduate from that old school building. Diana was on the leading edge of the baby boom, several months older than most of her classmates. The city fathers recognized the bulging demographic shifts as her age group approached their teen years, and they funded construction of a futuristic, sprawling new complex to be called Paul G. Blazer High School. When it was finished in the months prior to her senior year, it would stand on dozens of thick concrete pylons, as though anticipating a typhoon and deep flood waters up there in the mountains.

Diana Judd developed into an attractive teenager with bright eyes and a fine complexion, as her high-school yearbook pictures prove. Small framed, she developed early. Despite her extraordinarily active imagination and dramatics, she was basically a conformist as a teen. She kept her studies up and involved herself in extracurricular activities, but even within her immediate peer group she remembers herself as shy.

"I was always extremely shy," Naomi said. "They always

called me the China Doll because I was very fragile and had the porcelain skin. And I made straight A's. I wanted to be liked, so I got along with everybody from the cheerleaders to the delinquents."

Shy or not, she was popular with the boys. When she was fourteen she met one particular boy, Michael Ciminella, Jr., on a blind date. Ciminella was two years older, extremely bright, glib, fast, and exciting. He has credited his Italian Catholic heritage for a personality that includes both extreme sensitivity and a fiery temperament. He was the son of a well-heeled family that had moved to Ashland from his birthplace in Erie, Pennsylvania. His social standing was farther up the ladder than Diana's. There are indications that some in his family disapproved of his continuing attentions to the service station owner's beautiful young daughter. Mike Ciminella, Sr., owned Ashland Aluminum Products, and the family belonged to the Bellefonte Country Club, the place where the most important people in the local social scene enjoyed themselves in exclusive surroundings.

"Naomi was no stranger to the dances they held out at the country club every summer," said Russell Powell, recalling those early dates she had with Ciminella. "We all went to them. They had a band, and they were really the thing."

Naomi recalls her childhood and adolescence in Ashland as an idyllic time, surrounded as she was by a family of Waltons-like closeness in a small town with the virtues of Andy Griffith's Mayberry. She gained values both real and romanticized from that period that color her view of her life and career even today.

"Ashland is our home," Naomi said. "Wynonna and I were born right there in King's Daughters'. Those people are our family and friends. They mean more to us than anyone in the world.

"When you come from small-town Middle America, like

Ashland, Kentucky, and you know what holds water, what's important in life, and you have a respect for your priorities, it gives you an inner self-confidence that is one of the most valuable assets a human being can have."

Of course, even Sheriff Andy left Mayberry for a better career opportunity in Cleveland, Ohio. The truth about all small towns is that they are, for gypsy souls and adventurous people, wonderful places to have come from.

"Ashland is one of those small towns that everybody's dying to get out of," Naomi confessed in a less nostalgic moment. Because of that, she wound up with interesting friends from high school dispersed all around the country, including Noah Adams of National Public Radio's "All Things Considered" fame. "They are scattered across the U.S., and I'm the walking class reunion."

The local hangout for teens when Diana turned seventeen was the Bluegrass Grill. Favorite songs on the car radio would have included the electrifying smoothness of Sam Cooke, Brook Benton, and Martha and the Vandellas. The Beatles and the British invasion were another twelve months away.

On her seventeenth birthday, with the image of politics in the weekly photo magazines such as *Life*, the *Saturday Evening Post*, and *Time*, America was floating in a celebration of youth and vigor, as touch football games on the White House lawn and the sophisticated fashions of the Kennedy women perpetuated the beautiful myth of Camelot.

Naomi characterizes Diana Ellen Judd as a sheltered Pollyanna in her late teens, innocent and blissfully ignorant of the possibility that one wrong step or one unlucky roll of the dice could change forever her easy world. Smart, attractive, popular, and insulated from harm by Polly's best intentions, Diana was a happy teenager.

Her relationship with Mike Ciminella had continued off

and on after that first blind date when she was fourteen. When he graduated from high school, though, he was accepted as a science student at Georgia Tech and left her far, far away in her junior year. He didn't stay in Georgia long. By his sophomore year he had transferred closer to home to one of Kentucky's prestigious private schools, Transylvania College in Lexington. He was home for the summer of 1963 between his first and second years of college, and he and Diana were seeing quite a lot of each other. He told her of his plans when he finished his degree work, a major in business management with minor emphasis in chemistry.

At the beginning of what promised to be yet another idyllic summer in Ashland, just before her senior year in high school, Diana didn't have plans she could articulate. Each new year added to her feeling of being special, a typical idea among oldest children, and to a vague desire to do something both exciting and out of the ordinary with her life. Her high-school extracurricular activities had included membership in the student council and speech club her sophomore year. She was part of the school-sponsored Prayer Group and a member of the Y-Teens organization. She belonged to the service sorority, Theta Club, and served as both chaplain and vice president of her homeroom.

Service, religion, and a willingness to accept responsibilities are traits that even the young Diana Judd possessed. But had you asked her of her plans for the future at the beginning of that summer vacation, she would probably have answered with a blithe shrug of her shoulders and an invitation to go swimming with her and her closest friend, her brother Brian.

One afternoon that summer, after they had gone swimming together, Diana and Brian bounded through the front door of the big two-story Judd house still in their swim suits. When Brian pulled the towel off his shoulders, his mother noticed a large lump on one of his shoulders. Brian was a hard worker, hustling two paper routes every afternoon, so Diana thought that the lump was just a big callus grown under the canvas strap of her brother's newspaper bag. Their mother knew better.

Polly called their family doctor immediately, and it didn't take long for him to bring back to the tight-knit family the news that would devastate each member, push Diana further into her boyfriend's comforting arms than either of them really were prepared for, and eventually destroy Polly and Glen Judd's marriage. At fifteen, Brian had a particularly virulent form of lymphatic cancer known as Hodgkin's disease. There was no cure.

Actually headed by Polly Judd, the family had always followed her soft-spoken, reserved behavior and relied on her for strength. With the sudden death sentence pronounced on her son, Polly Judd went to pieces, crying in her bedroom, so that the children could hear her down the hall. Diana was as stunned and frightened by the sounds of her mother's hysterical sobbing as she was by the news that Brian was seriously ill.

There is a cancer treatment center literally around the block from Naomi's childhood home now, but in 1963 that was not the case. Polly and Glen left their children at home alone on the night that they found out about Brian's cancer diagnosis. They were gone a great deal of the next two years, desperately seeking specialists who could offer some hope, some exotic treatment that might make a lie of the death sentence implicit in the original diagnosis. Diana, as the oldest child, tried to fill her parent's shoes, getting help from friends, neighbors, and family in raising younger sister Margaret and younger brother Mark, but the load on her was tremendous. The stress was something that she was simply too young and inexperienced to cope with.

It was made worse by the family's inability to openly face

Brian's illness. Polly and Glen refused to believe that their son was going to die. There was a perverse strain in the air when Polly and Glen were there. The subject was simply not allowed to come up. Much of the time the three of them— Glen, Polly, and Brian—were off at some cancer clinic or chasing after some oncologist with a reputation for trying new things, hoping against hope to get help. It was depressing for the whole family.

Diana's piano teacher chided her for coming to lessons unprepared. There was so much for her to do around the house with her mother gone—laundry, meals, relatives poking their heads in constantly, not to mention her own mental anguish. Practicing the piano was near the bottom of her list of priorities. Under her own strains and without her mother's constant menacing encouragement to mind that "Jesus and germs" were everywhere, she soon fell away from the church and playing piano for the Baptist children's Sunday school.

"I was about to lose my mind," she said. "I had no one to turn to."

Bottled up with frustration and denied the consolation of sharing her feelings about Brian with her family, Diana clung to Mike Ciminella, an "older man" with a strong shoulder to cry on. Everything else in her world seemed to have turned to hard work, gloom, and insecurity. Ciminella offered comfort and forbidden excitement.

When Mike Ciminella packed his bags in 1962 for a freshman year at Georgia Tech, he took along a growing affection for Diana. He brought it back with him to Transylvania, stoked by the relative ease with which he could fetch her up to Lexington for a fraternity weekend, or return home for a country-club dance. Mike joined Kappa Alpha fraternity, and friends from those days remember him as quite socially active, though it was understood that he had a "steady" back home, whom he often brought over for a big event like KA's annual formal, the Old South Ball.

"Mike was real popular, and there were a lot of girls interested in dating him at school," said Lexington radio sports personality and former Kappa Alpha fraternity brother Billy Reed. "But they said that he had this real good-looking girlfriend back in Ashland, and that seemed to be that."

There was more there than met the eye.

T·W·O

The Dark Road
Through Hollywood

Mike and Diana eloped.

"It's a teenage tragedy story," Wynonna told the Phoenix *Republic*. "They fell madly in love, had to get married—and back then it didn't work."

It had been a nervous Christmas and New Year's break from school for Mike and Diana. She was four months along —there was no way to postpone a decision any longer. As small as Diana was, her pregnancy had begun to show early in the school year. Embarrassed school authorities put off censure as long as they could. After talking about it and undoubtedly suffering the suggestions of their respective parents throughout the holidays, they finally decided to "do the right thing."

It was a slow-moving Friday in the dead of winter, January 3, 1964, as Diana and Mike drove east across the mountains to Pearisburg, the county seat of Giles County, Virginia. Mike was nineteen; in only eight days Diana would reach her eighteenth birthday, but it was no longer a question of waiting. They went to the circuit court clerk's office for same-day service on their marriage license. It had been a short work-week for the county, interrupted in the middle by New Year's Day. The clerk wasn't even in when the two scared but determined Kentucky teens entered the office. The assistant clerk took their information and issued the license.

They could have been married by a judge at the court-house if they could have found one, but Diana preferred to have religious sanction for their union. Mike obliged his bride-to-be and drove around Pearisburg, a veritable blip on the map with only twenty-one hundred citizens, until they located Baptist minister Rev. R. D. McGrady to perform the brief, private ceremony. There wasn't much to do in Giles County on a cold Friday night, or any other time for that matter, but the young newlyweds weren't in much of a mood for celebrating anyway. They drove home. It wasn't a very romantic honeymoon. A few days later, Mike was due back in Lexington to start the new college term at Transylvania.

"We all make mistakes," Naomi said, recalling that un-avoidable January wedding day. "I made my mistakes when I was a teenager—I got married when I was seventeen. You can't top that one."

They were married, but no one was particularly pleased. For the Ciminellas, there was the rub that the Catholic church didn't recognize any marriage except that performed by a priest. Diana didn't like what little she knew about Catholics and would never have signed the prenuptial agree-ment then required of a non-Catholic, promising that any children would be raised in the Catholic church. Quiet re-sentments had to be swallowed.

At the start of 1964, adjustments to the reality of the marriage presented themselves and accommodations were made. Mike was still a student, with business management taking precedence over chemistry as the focus of his studies, but it was hard to keep his mind on that. As an unemployed undergraduate he was in no position to support his wife. His parents were.

Diana moved out of her own family's home and into the Ciminellas as a newlywed. The family hired a tutor for her, the same one who was working with homebound cancer patient Brian Judd.

Public morality in a small town being what it was in the early sixties, Diana Ciminella, no matter that she now was respectably married, found it impossible to return to classes at Paul G. Blazer High School as her pregnancy continued healthily to term. No matter what dislocations she might experience because of this coming child, Diana looked forward to giving birth that spring.

Diana's senior-class picture shows a more mature and circumspect young woman than the shy and untroubled beauty reflected in former years' annuals. She applied a false beauty mark to her right cheek and whipped her hair under in contrast to the carefree, bouncy, flipped-up curl of previous years. Much of that year found Diana in a kind of limbo, alternately happy and sad.

Removed from the familiarity of her parents' house, she had plopped down in the middle of a family that masked their resentment of her precipitous and early marriage to their son. Despite their ample support for her and the coming child, Diana had a lot of emotions to sort through. These were a bittersweet mixture of optimistic expectations and subtle tensions.

On the positive side, Diana was very much in love with Mike Ciminella and looking forward to becoming a mother. Marriage at long distance gets difficult after a while, but Diana knew that after the baby was born, mother and child would be joining Mike in an off-campus apartment in Lexington by the start of classes in the fall of 1964. Mary Ciminella gave her perky young daughter-in-law lessons in what Diana termed Homemaking 101 to pass the time.

Her new life was tempered by Brian's illness and the gathering storms at her family's home. The marriage hadn't removed the strain of her brother's continued sickness or of seeing her parents drifting apart from their own pain and frustration. When Brian's disease was first diagnosed, Diana had tried to shoulder parental responsibility for her siblings Mark and Margaret. At seventeen, though, she was mostly a sheltered woman-child herself. It was a terrible strain on her. Now she was eighteen and expecting. She has told of studying at her parents' house with Brian and their tutor, but she couldn't do much for her mother now that she wasn't living there. The Judd household was in an uproar. It may have appeared stoic from the outside, but it would continue to be tense and unsettled up to and beyond the day when cancer finally claimed the life of Brian Judd in 1965.

"My brother died a tragic death," Naomi explained. "My mom and dad both went kind of crazy, you know. Sometimes tragedy bonds people, and sometimes it tears them apart."

Frustration and financial pressures mounted from traveling around the country chasing a string of faint hopes that inevitably failed. Glen Judd still had to oversee operations at the biggest and busiest service station in the booming little town. He turned to alcohol for relief. That wasn't the kind of development that a hard-shell Baptist Sunday school teacher was going to abide with any great equanimity. It was as though the cancer that had eaten away Brian Judd's health was more slowly and insidiously beginning through that winter to eat away at Glen and Polly's relationship.

About four hundred Ashland teenagers walked in caps and gowns through the first commencement celebrated at Paul Blazer in late May of 1964. They sang the alma mater, threw their mortar board caps in the air at the end, and signed each other's yearbooks with pledges of eternal fealty and friendship. Diana Ciminella, though she had completed her studies with the tutor, didn't participate in this commencement exercise. She had experienced a graduation all her own about a week earlier. She had gone to King's Daughters' medical center, the scene of her own birth, to become a mother herself. While her classmates sang the strains of the school song, Diana responded contentedly to the hungry warblings of Christina Claire Ciminella. The future Miss Wynonna Judd was trying out her voice.

With the help of the senior Ciminellas, arrangements were made in Lexington for comfortable accommodations for the young family. September 1964 rolled around, and Mike began his third year of college. Friends from those college and newlywed days recall Mike and Diana at fraternity functions, but Diana was somewhat intimidated by that scene and was not remembered as the talkative and flamboyant person that she is today.

Even with the baby to care for, Diana determined to attempt college on her own. Rather than crowd Mike at Transylvania, she opted to attend the University of Kentucky main campus at Lexington. She began taking courses there as a part-time student in the fall semester of 1964. The demands of marriage and child-rearing overwhelmed her by 1966 and she quit school, nowhere near a bachelor's degree.

As the baby grew chubby cheeked and healthy, there were ample opportunities to see the beautiful bluegrass horse farms that were at every edge of Lexington, though the city has now grown to engulf them. Thoroughbred horses running through rolling green pastures surrounded by neatly maintained white wooden fences stirred something in Mike Ciminella. The muscular grace of the horses and the luxuriant gentility of manicured pastures would bring him back to Lexington and the thoroughbred business years later—by himself.

It took Mike five years to earn his bachelor's degree. The transfer from Georgia Tech, added to the switch from a science to a business major, cost him two extra semesters' work. But he finally graduated from Transylvania with a bachelor of arts in business administration in 1967 and accepted a job offer in California, where he intended to go to graduate school. Three-year-old daughter Christina may have waved at her daddy as he walked up the platform in his cap and gown to accept his degree. She developed a close and affectionate relationship with her father.

If the father-daughter relationship developed naturally into an affectionate one, the husband-wife relationship took another, quite predictable course. Soon after she actually began living with Mike Ciminella, Diana began to suspect just how much of a sham marriage she had gotten herself into. Parental expectations and pressures from both sides pushed in at her, pressing her to "make it work for the child's sake" if for no other reason. Motherhood suited Diana to a tee, but the regular frictions and compromises of her marriage were another thing. People tend to grow into their own upbringings as they reach their points of maturity. That's when people can find out just how different they are from each other. During those years, Diana and Mike were expected to grow up early.

Mike Ciminellas' family and social background imparted higher expectations than did the Glen Judd household. Mike's family encouraged accomplishment in business, including the social obligations that success entails, whereas Polly's lessons leaned more toward conforming to a domestic career, with a stiff dose of Baptist theology. Although Mike thrived in his expected adult role as a business success, Diana chafed under all but the mothering part of hers. Time passed, and the cumulative mental growth of higher education began to mold Mike's self-confidence and goals. He seemed almost daily to inch ahead of her.

Mike's future in California was very promising, indeed. At the beginning of the 1960s President Kennedy set the United States on a course to conquer outer space. The NASA program accelerated from the single-astronaut vehicles of the Mercury program to the two-man capsules of the Gemini program. This was all in preparation for the Apollo space launches in the late sixties that would lead America to land the first man on the moon, barely a year after Mike and Diana first set foot in Los Angeles. It was a hot time for the booming aerospace business, which possessed a cachet and glamour not entirely unlike that of Hollywood's film community. That's what Mike had gotten himself into.

"I went out and worked in aerospace electronics marketing and took my MBA courses in night school at UCLA," said Ciminella.

There was one change in their lives that Diana took with her when they moved.

"[Mike had] got out of college, and the company he worked for sent us out there," said Naomi of the California move. "When we landed I was pregnant with Ashley, so I actually had Ashley in Los Angeles."

On April 19, 1968, just after they moved from Lexington to the Los Angeles area, Ashley Tyler Ciminella was born. Christina was about four years old. Physically, Ashley would grow to resemble her mother even more than her older sister. Ashley was smaller framed and by her early teens would become devastatingly, achingly cute, rather than share the smoky handsomeness that Christina would acquire.

There was already uneasiness in the Ciminellas' marriage. In anticipating the California move, it is a remarkable quality of youth that both of them probably thought that the change of scenery might allow them both to "grow into" each other's lives more. California seemed like such a promising place.

For Diana, the move meant exposure to the truly cosmopolitan atmosphere of Los Angeles. The Beach Boys sang of endless summers by the ocean, and the fan magazines painted splashy pictures of Hollywood's glitz and glamour. And Diana would, for once, be out of the immediate range of their parents.

California was about as far from Ashland, Kentucky, in culture and scenery as one can imagine, especially in 1968. Psychedelic music, art, and drugs were creating a youth culture that the whole country was eager to emulate. Subculture manifestations bloomed in more varieties than Baskin-Robbins has of ice cream. If the "peace, love, and find your own thing" aspects of the youth movement didn't appeal to Diana, the freedom and color of the pageant certainly captured her imagination.

"When we first moved to Hollywood, I learned how to delineate an astrological chart," she explained. "I went to the theosophical society and found out how to cast a horoscope. I've always been one of these that wants to find out for myself. I wanted to find out if it was just arcane flapdoodle or pre-science science."

The outpouring of creativity and the philosophical movement toward recapturing the primitive, natural simplicity of Thoreau's *Walden* also began to appeal to the awestruck young Kentucky woman. Her interest was piqued by the concept of a vegetarian diet, the latest fad. In California, many people who had never seen the inside of an outhouse were talking about the virtues of rural simplicity. Few of that kind were among Mike Ciminella's cohorts, mind you. These were Diana's interests.

And then there was the more traditional glamour of the Hollywood area, where abject sleaze mixed with the celluloid dreams that fairly boiled off the rooftops of major film studios. Diana had been one of the prettiest girls in Ashland, but that was a small fish bowl indeed.

"I had never really been out of Ashland except maybe to go to Myrtle Beach for a week in the summer with my family," she said.

To her surprise and gratification, she turned out to be beautiful in Los Angeles, too. Hers were the good looks of a cover girl, the fresh-scrubbed sex appeal of a petite Playboy bunny. But what to do about it? There must be someplace for her among all the opportunities she imagined were around like plums to be plucked.

Hollywood, of course, had hardly been sitting around on its collective behind holding its breath for the arrival of the prettiest girl from Ashland, Kentucky. In fact, her affected southernisms and her favorite down-home Kentucky expressions didn't go over particularly well on the hip West Coast. Diana found out the hard way that eastern Kentucky was pretty far off the beaten path of the rest of the world. Putting on her "country face" with purposely exaggerated folk expressions like "slap the dog and spit in the fire" went down smoothly on Little Cat Creek but was more likely to garner cat calls among the California "hips" or the educated elite of Mike Ciminella's aerospace advertising business.

Diana liked her new surroundings but didn't want her daughters to lose touch with their "real" home. Often, when school was finished for the year, the girls returned to Ashland for a summer vacation with their grandparents. Ashley was really too young to appreciate the contrasts, but Christina got a renewed dose of that small-town Kentucky culture. From the corner of Hollywood and Vine to the beveled-glass front door of Polly Judd's house is a gap that takes more than miles to measure. Christina loved to hang around her grandfather Judd's service station as much as her mother had as a child.

"I used to work there kind of in the summer time," Wynonna said. "When we lived in Hollywood I used to always go back to Kentucky for the summer and help him pump gas and stuff."

"That's where I grew up," Naomi interrupted. "There's a pinball machine in there that I could work . . . I knew I was grown up when I didn't have to stand on a pop case to reach the tilt button."

"We were living out in Hollywood, and you can imagine what it was like," Wynonna continued. "I used to walk past the Nine Thousand Building; the Whiskey A Go Go and the Roxy were just down the street. Ashley and I would fly back and stay the whole summer visiting Aunt Polly and Uncle Landon out on their farm. They had a well and a pump in the kitchen, but it was just cold water."

Christina was also a regular at grandma Ciminella's summer luncheons at the Bellefonte Country Club, but it was nothing like the restaurants she could stare at, if not afford to go into, back in California. The contrasts reinforced Wynonna's concept of having come from somewhere special, homey, conservative, and self-sustaining.

"Those seven years in Hollywood made us realize what we had," Naomi told Nashville reporter Bob Oermann in the *Tennessean*. "When we went out there, I thought everybody had an Aunt Zora who had never taken a bath in her life, that everybody knew what a copperhead looked like and how to chop its head off. People made fun of the way we talked. At first I was real embarrassed. I got real quiet. I thought about what I was going to say and wouldn't use any colorful, crazy southern expressions. I had been very sheltered."

For a long time there was within that relationship more semblance of normality than one might gather from some of the foreboding descriptions of that time. There were stimulating people to meet, such as famed Western novelist Louis L'Amour. L'Amour's daughter became a friend to Christina. There were other children of notables around for Christina to associate with, including at least one child of a famous movie star in Christina's Brownie Scout troop.

"I was old fashioned and had a Brownie troop with one of my members being Jayne Mansfield's daughter," Naomi said. "Wynonna's best friend in school was Angelique L'Amour, the daughter of Western novelist Louis L'Amour."

Though she had a few college credits under her belt, Diana had no job skills. Neither did she have the social reach to match Ciminella's crowd. There she was in the middle of the motion picture capital of the world, with her only assets good looks and a yen to be different. But, that was a powerful yen, and her vision of her life was beginning to diverge considerably from her husband's.

"I loved being a mother, but I hated marriage," she said. "I realized I didn't know what I was doing when I was eighteen years old. There was a whole other world out there."

Of course, Ciminella was making good money and his MBA studies promised to deliver him into even higher-paid managerial levels, but that would be his accomplishment, not Diana's. For all her small-town, middle-class upbringing, she had a streak of rambunctious country girl in her. Playing the discreet wifey to Ciminella's rising young businessman was not her idea of what life was all about. Away from the constraints and limitations of Ashland, Diana was growing in self-confidence and chafing at the frictions between her rising adventurousness and her husband's cynical rationalism. Ciminella is polite and considerate, but both he and Diana had tempers. They both had stubborn streaks and as they reached their midtwenties each began to admit that their dreams and ambitions were pulling them in separate directions.

Neither her Baptist upbringing nor his Roman Catholic background recommended divorce, which is one reason, Diana says, that they stayed together as long as they did. In the final accounting, the change of scene to California did not work any magic on Diana and Mike's relationship. She has called the years of her marriage to Ciminella "the darkest years" of her life. Her tendency to dramatize may have made the actual occurrences of those years seem somewhat more heinous than they might have appeared to an impartial observer, but it nonetheless colored her experience in very real ways. Things boiled under the surface until she could no longer keep the lid on her feelings.

"I think it took getting away from Kentucky to give me the courage to get a divorce," Naomi said. "I was so guilt ridden, belonging to the church and not being happy with our marriage."

In the end, she said, conditions became unbearable. She had finally gotten old enough to realize that it was her life she was wasting and not those of the Judd or Ciminella family members who would oppose the breakup. It was the 1970s already, and she was no longer a malleable teenager. She had become a headstrong grown woman, a woman as stubborn as her mother, though in different ways. Her time had come, and she had no further interest in hanging on to a deteriorating marriage, the way her own mother continued to do back home in Ashland.

"I was tired of being a martyr," she said. "I knew it wasn't healthy for the kids. I got out there, didn't know anybody, didn't have any family around me, and finally got up the nerve to make the split."

In June of 1972, when Ashley was four and Christina was eight, Diana filed for a divorce. She and Mike had separated at her insistence, and during the summer they worked out terms for a divorce settlement that included who would get what car and how the children were to be taken care of. The terms were quite generous to Diana, but then, she had dictated the terms to a lawyer neighbor. Ciminella agreed to let the proceedings go forward in default so that he wouldn't have to appear in court. It was an ordeal he simply didn't wish to face. He expected that Diana, who was acting as her own attorney, could get the simple facts before the court in December for the interlocutory decree, the step before the final dissolution of a marriage in the California legal system. He figured that she would follow up on filing the petition to make their divorce final six months after that, since she wanted this divorce so god-awful much. He left his MBA studies unfinished at UCLA, and the company he worked for transferred him to Chicago.

They had to tell the court that they had been separated for exactly one year, though the divorce had likely been a much more compulsive decision when Diana finally screwed up the nerve to tell Michael she wanted out—had not all these years in fact, wanted to be married.

When Diana went to court a few weeks before Christmas, the balmy Los Angeles weather belied the seasonal spirit that she had grown up with, of cold rainy days and cedar trees' pungent odor in the living room. She didn't ask for alimony; she was ready to strike out on her own. When she left the courthouse that day, she had earned her interlocutory decree, setting the terms of the divorce settlement, if not the final divorce itself, in force.

Interlocutory decrees state on their faces what the court requires of petitioners in a divorce. Couples must wait six months, then petition again for the final decree. Otherwise the court reserves the right to decide of its own volition in the absence of protests to the contrary. Diana read that and expected that it would do just that. She washed her hands of the matter and left it to the course of natural events. But then, sometimes the Los Angeles Superior Court has more important things to do with its time than read people's minds, and sometimes half-finished paperwork gets put away in a file and forgotten.

Diana got Ciminella to enter into a binding legal agreement to pay her an amount slightly exceeding 25 percent of his monthly income in support of Christina and Ashley. At the time it was barely enough for a decent apartment in Los Angeles, though it would be a tidy sum in a less expensive town. There was even a requirement that if he got a raise in salary, she would get a raise in child support. To make sure that his children's health would be seen to, he agreed to keep them on his major medical insurance and pay any expenses not covered, including dental. Looking ahead, Ciminella also agreed to pay college expenses and tuition for both girls. Throw in a year-old Chevrolet for Diana, and you have a more than decent settlement, even in an otherwise demanding community-property state like California.

Naomi has been loath to discuss the problems that led to their filing for divorce, either publicly or privately, though she has hinted broadly at some awful, dark, brooding secret between them. On the other hand, Ciminella, about whom so much has been hinted by his ex-wife, seemed ready to clear the air on that subject.

"We had some disagreements about several things in our marriage," Mike Ciminella, Jr., explained. "We finally mutually agreed to get a divorce and go our separate ways. It was a very amicable thing. We used our next-door neighbor who was an attorney, and I think it cost us sixteen dollars and whatever it cost to Xerox the papers involved. It was not one of those big whizzing contests that some people get into. We just had very different interests and agreed to pursue our different interests after the split."

So much for deep, dark secrets. There was a pause, then a questioning chuckle from him.

"Does that conflict with something else you may have heard about me?" he asked. "That doesn't surprise me. I think that that arose because I was very successful after we split and she wasn't. Not for a long time. Not until just recently, really. As far as the success of the Judds, I think that is a fifty-fifty split between her (Diana's) tenacity, and Christina's ability to hit the high notes. I don't think either one of them could have made it without the other."

Diana and her two girls stayed in the Los Angeles area, in her not-so-nice apartment in the Hollywood section. The stability of the marriage was gone, and so was the luxury of being supported by a marketing executive on the rise. Her father's Los Angeles home, Wynonna told one reporter, had been decked out with "three TVs, two refrigerators and four telephones." Not so Diana's first Hollywood apartment.

One apartment she and the two girls initially inhabited during that time has been described as a poorly furnished flat next door to a post office. Later, when the Judds were famous, Naomi would look out the window of a Hollywood hotel room and cry when she spotted "the run down little house where we used to live on Sunset Boulevard."

"So here I was, high and dry in Hollywood," Naomi recalled. "I went to West Hollywood Community Church even though I worked two jobs at a time, and went without sleep practically. I was just trying to put food in my kids' bellies and keep a roof over our heads, and it was a struggle. But at the same time, it was the price you pay for freedom. You know, if the watermelon falls off the truck, it ain't gonna get up by itself. You've got to help it out. You've got to participate in your life."

She was on her own, but because of the girls there could never be a time when she would not be in some kind of communication with her ex-husband. She has told stories of continuing troubles with Ciminella after they split, run-ins that apparently did nothing to make her life any easier.

"I mean, there were times when I really wondered what I was doing," she explained to the Houston *Chronicle*. "One day Wynonna was sick; I don't know what was wrong with her. We didn't have a car—my ex-husband was throwing his weight around and took our only car—and I had to take her to the doctor. She was six or seven years old, a big kid, and I was carrying her. She was burning up with fever and I was thinking, 'My God, what in the world!' "

The breakup of the Ciminella family had costs for others besides Diana. The loss of her father was hard on Christina, who at eight could begin to grasp snippets of the foul emotions that swirl around even an amicable breakup. Nothing that ends in divorce can really be all that amicable, regardless of the civility of an uncontested settlement. Ashley, as a four-year-old, understood nothing of the relief of legal separation felt by the adults who could no longer abide living under the same roof with each other.

Christina was fond of junk food and many of the other trappings of her "Valley girl" existence before her parents broke up. With her father gone to Chicago and their standard of living reduced, the girl became an afternoon junk food binger. When she got out of West Hollywood Elementary School, she walked home to a life of fattening snacks and mindless television. She made friends in her new neighborhood and showed few outward signs of maladjustment, besides weight gains, but she was deeply wounded. There was an emptiness in her world.

To the extent that she could, Diana maintained continuity for her children. She went from being a full-time mother to working several jobs at a time, so the mother-daughter communication shifted to one of "love notes and Twinkies." Always a fiercely protective mother, she didn't trust Hollywood enough to let her daughters become latchkey children, so each day after school they reported to the generous supervision of friendly neighborhood families.

As the new reality of living in a broken home sunk in, Christina tried to hold onto those elements of her life that she could keep like the old days. Hollywood was the original "fast lane," so in becoming the child of a broken home she had come closer to the norm there.

Even with the privation of being without a car for a short while in a city as stretched out as the Los Angeles area, there were benefits to Diana and her children from being there. For one thing, she knew her girls were being exposed to a high-quality education in the California school system, and she wanted to give herself a chance to cut a niche in something more glamorous than secretarial work.

"One reason why I stayed was that the educational systems were better out there," Naomi admitted. "Wynonna did wonderfully well. She got double promoted. She made straight A's, and there are so many opportunities out there; so many interesting jobs."

Partly out of homesickness, Diana taught her daughters old folk songs and old hymns that she remembered from her own childhood during their Hollywood years.

If there was a glimmer in anybody's mind that these family sing-alongs might portend a place for either of them in show business, it was certainly not apparent to Christina. "Growing up in L.A. I don't remember a radio or even music being a priority in the house," she said.

Los Angeles was good for the girls, but it held promise for Diana, too. Diana had dreams, vague ones to be sure, but they were prime motivators for the decision to stay on. Her finances and her emotions were disorganized right after she split with Ciminella. To find her first job after her divorce, she answered an ad for receptionist for the Fifth Dimension. It was a short-lived job, replacing a woman on leave to have a baby.

Diana wasn't really interested in a single mundane job; she preferred to hold several part-time jobs instead. One of Diana's favorite part-time jobs added hip, trendy concepts to her nostalgic view of her "old Kentucky home." She tells of being a clerk in a snazzy seeds-and-stems natural food store called the Golden Carrot, down off Sunset Boulevard. Lots of back-to-basics types—slick business people into hip "whole grain" trends as well as genuine crumbs-in-their-beards hippie dropouts—shopped there. Ever the adventurous soul, Diana adopted a meatless diet to see if it really would keep her healthier. She also developed an interest in such herbal cures as tree-bark tea in place of aspirin. Such natural cures were right out of the rural Boyd County medicine cabinet.

She says that she found a kind of stability when she went to work for millionaire philanthropist Ben Abner, for whom she worked for the next year and a half.

"I gave away his money," Naomi said. "He had some kids and they had trust funds. He had a yacht and an apartment down at Marina del Rey. I had all these bills to pay. I did all of his household stuff. I hired his household staff."

Abner was good to her and her children.

"I remember going there on weekends," Wynonna recalled of her mother's generous employer. "She'd work there on weekends to take care of his books. I remember he had a swimming pool with steps all the way down from his house with marble floors. It was just incredible."

From Abner, she next hooked up with oriental millionaire David Chou. Chou's requirements didn't keep her forty hours a week either, so she continued to find outside work. The best paying of these additional positions was modeling.

"It was just an accident," she said of her fortuitous chance to begin a career. "A guy up the street was the head of the photography department for the Arts Center School of Design and asked if I would do a session with him. It was relatively good money for a girl who didn't have anything but a high-school diploma. That got me a bunch of pictures. I bought one of those little portfolios and then—bingo—I became a successful model."

Other, less savory opportunities were presented to her, as well. A pretty, young divorcée with two children is fair game for the wolves of Hollywood unless she keeps her wits about her. As time passed, she became disenchanted with modeling, and though she had no experience to qualify her for any real acting jobs, a few were reportedly offered.

"One time, a big [film] producer who lived up the street put a script under the windshield wiper of my car, outlined in red the parts he wanted me to read," she said, illuminating her distaste for the sleazy undercurrents of California show business. "He'd seen me walking my kids down the street— you know?"

She had no stomach for the sexual quid pro quo that always seemed to be insinuated in offers to an inexperienced, would-be actress. Yet, inexperienced and semiskilled as she was, Diana Ciminella was nobody's fool.

As she began to get more modeling assignments, she found that her easiest source of big money was standing in front of a camera. There was always fierce competition for the best paying jobs, though. Usually when jobs came they were body-parts shots, with her feet modeling shoes for a mail-order catalog, for instance.

"I could earn more money in a three-hour [photo] shoot

than I could make in a forty-hour week as a secretary," she explained.

The money was great, but when it came to the nitty-gritty, she just couldn't stay in the ring. Diana was incensed by the reality of the brutally competitive modeling circuit. She had the good looks for it, but not the personality, as she tells the story.

"It's vacuous," she reported about modeling. "It's vanity. I never felt comfortable with it. In fact, I walked out of [an audition for] a Maybelline commercial . . . It was real cut-throat, and these girls would freak out if they broke a nail."

As much as despising what modeling was, Diana hated it for what it was not. It wasn't mentally stimulating or satisfying in any way other than monetarily.

"I hated the modeling professions because I didn't think I was doing anything of service or anything I could be proud of," she said. "I hated depending on my looks for my living. I wasn't doing anything with my mind and I wasn't helping anybody."

Of course, there were some offers that came looking for her. Sometimes there were offers of quick cash for a nude spread. Whether the photographers actually represented the publications they claimed to or were just free-lancing, some told her they could get her into the biggest men's magazines.

Naomi is not a shy woman; she has never claimed to be. "I'm divorced and I've been to the circus and I've seen the clowns," as she put it. "This ain't my first rodeo."

But neither is she one who will allow men to take advantage of her. Despite being in what she has painted as sometimes desperate financial straits, she remained fully in control of her own sexual destiny. No fly-by-night photographer was going to put one over on her with vague promises of "I'll make you a star." They grossly underestimated her intelligence with that approach. She was usually attracted to men who seemed willing to help, but she could readily see the difference. She may use her good looks to her own best advantage, but she is nobody's bimbo and nobody's bumpkin.

"I used to get propositions from *Penthouse* and *Playboy* all the time, but that was just so . . . ," she struggled for words. "I didn't even have to think twice about that [even though] I worked two jobs out there just to pay the rent and there were some really, really lean times."

After a couple of years as a single mother, Diana found that Hollywood began to wear thin. A string of part-time jobs anchored around the stability of the Abner and Chou positions came and went fairly fast, and she wasn't willing to toughen up her psyche to capitalize on her modeling opportunities. Naomi has told vaguely of working for a video production company and an insurance agency. Watching the world of Hollywood, she said, taught her something important about the value of her plain Kentucky upbringing. Money, although no doubt handy, didn't come with a guarantee of happiness.

"I saw how the rich lived and how money often compounded their problems," she said. "And how people are so busy falling for everything that they don't really stand for anything."

She decided that the men of Hollywood didn't hold enough interest for her, either. Another adjustment to life as an unmarried woman was returning to the "market," as it were. Diana explored the dating scene, but found it not to her liking. She says that she found actors too egotistical and shallow and learned to avoid them. Like moths drawn to a flame, well-to-do suitors occasionally took their best shot at gaining her favors. On the whole, she didn't trust them. She quickly decided that as a practice, she didn't care much for dating.

"I've always had men in my life," she explained. "First I

was Glen Judd's daughter, then I was Wynonna's father's wife, and I've been single, technically speaking, since 1971 or '72. I don't date. I have long-term, heavy-duty relationships. But I haven't been very lucky with men."

"She was sought after by some very wealthy men in Hollywood," Wynonna remembered. "But she's always kept a real strong sense of who she is and she cared more about us. She could have sent us off to grandparents and had the time of her life."

Diana began to tire of fending off advances from men she considered shallow and phony, if sometimes rich and powerful. The men who attracted her most had talent or were truly solicitous of her and her daughters, which she appreciated more than money or power.

She began thinking seriously about returning to Kentucky to expose her daughters to their Appalachian cultural heritage. Ciminella's monthly check would stretch a lot further back there. She was determined to relocate to a place that would give her maximum flexibility to fortify the genuine backwoods Kentucky atmosphere with a holistic health kick that emphasized home remedies and vegetarianism.

Suddenly, at the peak of her Hollywood success, Diana decided that it was time to get out.

"The kids were starting to think Hollywood was normal and that summers back home were just vacations," she said.

"All of a sudden, she decided this was no place to raise babies," Wynonna said. "Ashley was still real young. We lived in a nice house. I was a typical Hollywood kid, coming home, eating Ding Dongs and watching 'The Brady Bunch,' watching TV all day. . . . We gave everything away; everything except the necessities: toys, scrapbooks, and clothes."

Diana's feet simply got itchy to be moving on. In a dramatic move to break with her California life, she sold or gave away most of her not inconsiderable worldly possessions. She would end up back home in Kentucky, but with a head full of dreams, she first headed out to seek adventure.

"I did a bunch of checking out before we went to Kentucky," Naomi said. "I went to Austin, Texas, and got a job as a weather girl on KLBJ-TV station. We rented a house out in West Gibson. I auditioned and got the job, but I never actually worked. I stayed there for six weeks; we were there from the end of July through the month of August but never got on the air.

"I chickened out because of the heat," she confessed. "I made a deposit on a little old white frame house outside of town—you know, there's something about the cowboy mystique."

Her fascination with Indian culture pulled her back out west to Arizona next. She heard about a program that would show her a wide territory as a low-level quasi nurse. In northern Arizona, the White River Apache Indian reservation had a desperate need for trained medical services personnel. She had always imagined herself as an Indian princess. She packed up and went to check it out.

"So I went to Arizona where I was assured a job working the circuit of the two hospitals in northeastern Arizona on an Apache reservation," she explained. "I was fascinated with the Indians. I thought it would be good for the kids to learn something about that part of America's crazy-quilt history," she said.

After a quick first-hand look around Arizona, however, she decided not to stay there either.

"The reason I didn't do it was because I couldn't subject my kids to their educational system," she said. "It was despicable."

When the Indian reservation didn't pan out, Diana decided to head home, to Kentucky, where she intended to get her nursing degree while soaking up Appalachian culture. She loaded up the girls one more time and drove off into the sunrise.

T·H·R·E·E

From Babylon to the Mountain Top

A lot had gone wrong for Diana. Her marriage was over. Men hit on her, and many of them turned out to be less than knights in shining armor. She did what she had to to get by, whatever it took, yet she still went from relative affluence as Ciminella's wife to semipoverty—by her own choice, but there it was nonetheless. All in all, Hollywood disappointed her. It could be phony and flaky, and sometimes both at the same time. Hollywood was not what she had dreamed it would be. The town had seen her at her best, and when she didn't tumble easily into its mold, it shrugged its shoulders and yawned "Next."

But where would home be for Diana now? There were problems with California, but there were just as surely drawbacks to going back home. She had seen and experienced a lot during the growing-up years of her twenties in Los Angeles. Many of Diana's peers had reveled in this free-spirited time, trying out drugs, Eastern religions, and other passing phases. She breathed in the spirit of the social climate, but she was no West Coast hippie. Diana was a Kentucky girl feeling her oats.

Without necessarily delving into all the manifestations of the 1960s, she let herself absorb energy from the changes going on around her. She had learned to appreciate the excitement of California, internalizing what she liked and rejecting the parts that wouldn't square with her basic values. There was no doubt that she was a different person from the exuberant eighteen-year-old new mother who left home for a crack at college and young family life in Lexington ten years before.

By 1974 there was a pall of bad energy affecting the so-called youth culture. It was a time of profound confusion for people who had built their egos in large part upon their opposition to the war in Vietnam and President Nixon. Having vanquished its foes in the war and the paranoid, sneaky Nixon administration, the protest generation was faced with the need to examine the values of free-wheeling life-styles to see if they held any meaning in the absence of cultural enemies.

Diana felt the shifting winds; they were unavoidable. But most important, she had to do the best thing for her children. She always tried to make her moves at the end of the school term. Her concern was for her daughters—that their gypsy life with her have as much continuity as possible.

Garnering the nerve to divorce Mike Ciminella freed her for the first time in her adult life to develop her sense of self-esteem. By living on her own and learning to work, she was proving something to herself. Establishing her independence began to relieve her of the constraints that Ashland and Polly Judd had chained her with before her confidence caught up with her good looks. As a teenager, the fact that she was attractive was the chief element in deciding her fate. She attracted a lusty young man and wound up married into the role she had been more or less bred for. In California, in the apex of the youth movement, she had become more assertive. Her self-discovery was to be a long and rambling process, but she would never look back with nostalgia for the old Diana.

So, there were choices to be made again. If she went back home to Ashland at that point she'd never hear the end of I-told-you-so's and well-intentioned meddling from the girls' grandparents. When the senior Ciminellas paid for Christina's piano lessons it wasn't meddling, but when the girls went home for a visit, Mike's parents took Christina to the country club and showed her a world Diana couldn't afford to give her. Christina had been there so much that she had picked out her favorite waitress among the women on staff.

With her mind set on leaving Hollywood, Diana made her plan, but this one was as loose as any when it came to the fine details. Rustication—getting back to the earth in quiet isolation—was on Diana's agenda. Her bottom line was to carve out a sensible future for herself by returning to Kentucky to pick up her education where it had left off some twelve years earlier. She hadn't given up on her dreams, but she no longer expected to give them substance in the shallow rat race of Hollywood, working from the ghetto of good looking would-be's turned off by modeling but unwilling to stay in the secretarial pool. Her practical goal was a better paying day job until fate called her number.

Once she decided to leave, her emerging life-style–philosophy helped dictate where she would eventually wind up on her cross-country journey. She needed something "country" in a sort of whole-grain organic manner. John Denver sang it all for a lot of people whose backgrounds were really rooted more in concrete and steel than in the Appalachian front-porch rocker in his 1971 hit "Take Me Home, Country

Wynonna and Naomi Judd. *(Beth Gwinn)*

Diana Judd in her senior picture, just before she married Mike Ciminella. *(Boyd County Library)*

Polly Judd's home in Ashland, where Diana was raised in middle-class comfort. *(Nashville Celebrity Research)*

1982 SENIOR

MOST TALENTED
Wynonna Judd
Chris McWhorter

On the verge of getting her big break, Wynonna was recognized by her classmates as the most talented girl in her senior class. *(Franklin High School)*

This comfortable two-story house, Chanticleer, was the Judds' country retreat in Morrill, Kentucky. Here's where Wynonna learned to play guitar and first started singing seriously with her mother. *(Nashville Celebrity Research)*

Wynonna's dreamy senior portrait. *(Franklin High School)*

Younger daughter Ashley went to Japan to work as a fashion model during her high-school summer vacation. *(Franklin High School)*

This is the first picture ever taken of Naomi and Wynnona in a recording studio together. The 1980 project was an attempt to record Wynonna alone, but it didn't work out. *(Jon Shulenberger)*

Roads." Diana's plan had everything: idealized rural living, not too far from her old hometown, in a place where she could slow down, hold the world at bay, and get a new start on life at the same time.

Ironically, in adapting her dreams to fit her immediate and most practical career move—nursing school—she would catch the first slight glimmer of what the future might hold for her and Christina.

Diana took care of her practical concerns first.

"I called the state board of nursing in Kentucky and asked them which college graduated girls in the highest percentile," Naomi explained.

When she got their report, she applied and was accepted to Eastern Kentucky University School of Nursing in Richmond.

Combining the practical goal of nursing with a desire to try an experiment in back-to-nature living gave her some parameters in looking for a home in Kentucky. Richmond was out: there was too much going on in that regional college town and the rents were too high for her budget. She wanted exposure to the culture, crafts, and art of the eastern Appalachian region. Berea is the only place organized as a focal point for these elements. Berea College Crafts—an offshoot of Berea College—was founded in 1893 and now has two hundred students working from traditional foundations in woodcraft, weaving, ceramics, needlecraft, and wrought iron. The arts, crafts, and music give the small town a rich atmosphere of creativity. After registering for her classes at EKU in the spring session of 1975, Diana and the girls drove down the road south a few miles from Richmond to Berea to look around for a place to live.

Berea proper, the midtown area that wraps itself around the stately brick buildings and expansive, well-cared-for lawns of Berea College, is an attractive place. The central part of this welcoming little college town is as quaint and colorful as the set for a full-blown production of the Broadway musical *The Music Man*. The city's tourist industry makes the most of the college's fame as an Appalachian craft center, of past regional connections to the legendary frontiersman Daniel Boone, and of the nearby "Renfro Valley Barn Dance," the once influential country music radio show that still operates each weekend.

There is a gracious country elegance about the town, an atmosphere of prosperity about its workaday inhabitants who stop in at the downtown druggists for a cherry cola or a root beer float made the old-fashioned way from behind the black deco fountain. In the well-tended neighborhoods that begin one block off the main square and down any of the several state roads that pass through Berea, one finds an appreciation for renovated old homes and genteel landscaping. If there is rough mountain poverty anywhere, it is well hidden.

Diana hit Berea looking for a cheap rent and a wholesome atmosphere in which to leave her two young daughters while she daily drove the fifteen miles up the road to EKU. She was eager for a quiet retreat, someplace far from the crowds of big-city California; someplace as far away from the world as possible.

"My idea of pleasure is kicking back at the end of the day, sitting on the porch, and listening to the crickets," she said. "I'm still looking for a place way back in the holler."

She needed to unwind, to calm down, to feel grass between her toes, and to try out an idealized countrified lifestyle, a good-earth simplicity that was beginning to appeal to a lot of young adults beat down toward cynicism by the political scandals of the seventies.

As for the need for retreat, hers was hardly an isolated case in the Berea area in the midseventies. The place in which she was going to live for the next two years was at that very moment a magnet for a relatively large number of drop-outs. People had come there from all over the country, but especially from California. Most either needed a quiet place to pull themselves back together or were moving into the mountainous countryside for life-style experiments such as the one Diana had in mind.

Diana spent several days looking for a decent place to live. She wanted her girls to have the benefit of Berea city schools, while also having the advantages (as she saw them; the girls would not immediately agree with her on this point) of exposure to a rural Kentucky heritage. Fate stepped in and simplified her search. In the course of touring the college itself, Diana stopped to be a Good Samaritan for Caroline Hovey, the wife of a Berea College music professor who had fallen and hurt her ankle. That simple act of caring for a stranger led to the most perfect rural living arrangements imaginable.

"When I met Diana she was looking for a place to live . . . with her two daughters," Caroline Hovey recalled. "I was running on campus because I was late to hear my husband's choir in their yearly concert. I hit a higher sidewalk and down I went. When I looked up there was a very beautiful lady looking over me.

"She was very kind to me and took me to the hospital emergency room. They stayed and waited for me; then they took me home and helped me into the house and up into my bed. They were really lovely people."

That story, combined with a report of the girls' housing plight, touched the heart of music teacher Margaret Allen. Mrs. Allen, a good friend of Caroline's, owned a huge pastoral estate in Morrill (pronounced "moral"), Kentucky, five miles outside Berea. She called her estate Windswept. Besides her own large house, there were five satellite houses named Ar-

den, Avalon, Paradise, Offspring and Chanticleer, the latter
being the largest and nicest of them. Each summer she
hosted student musicians in the houses for a two-week musical workshop. When Diana and the two little girls arrived,
Chanticleer was empty. For a very nominal rent the family
moved into the mountains just outside the Daniel Boone
National Forest where Jackson, Rockcastle, and Madison
counties intertwine like fingers folded in prayer.

Eleven-year-old Christina didn't consider the lonely hilltop to be such a religious experience at first.

"Having lived in California it was rough," Wynonna recalled. "I had spent summers in Kentucky, but there was still
a little culture shock when we moved."

Both Christina and Ashley considered themselves dis-
placed California kids. They had picked up at least the gloss
of worldliness and sophistication. Standing around Jack
Sparks's cozy little one-room grocery store–post office up in
Morrill swatting at summer flies and awaiting the mail was
nothing like haunting Sunset Boulevard after school.

Diana Ciminella went through several changes in her
life before she changed her name to Naomi Judd, but she
never did change her sense of being a mother lioness protect-
ing her two cubs. One of the first things she did was check out
Jackson County schools and decide that Ashley and Christina
would have to fake a Berea address so that they could attend
the vastly superior grammar schools in town.

Granny dresses and earth shoes became the uniform of
Diana's hilltop home, Chanticleer. She had a big time borrowing an ax to split kindling from the pile of fire wood
provided by Mrs. Allen at the side of the house. Although she
had been raised in comfortable middle-class surroundings,
Diana had been exposed to some elements of more rural
living among some Boyd County relatives, and she used her
active imagination to posit great virtue in living plain, with-

out amenities. She opted not to have a telephone, though Chanticleer was fully wired with electric power and phone lines, and had a two-car garage. If she had an old wringer washer on her back porch, it was because she wanted the experience of simplicity. Just two hours drive across I-64 from Ashland, Diana was getting back to nature, for the very first time.

"It was a very conscious decision on my part to live that way," Naomi said. "I wanted my daughters to be close to our family, close to our heritage. And I wanted my children to really learn where they came from, to have the freedom to develop their imaginations."

Her plan for her children worked out better than she could ever have guessed.

"All we had for entertainment was the radio, so I discovered music," Wynonna explained.

F·O·U·R

Life
on Bighill

Diana loved the roomy, two-story Chanticleer, located near the top of the highest peak in the area of prominence known locally as Bighill. The house itself is surrounded by a dozen apple, walnut, and shade trees, and berry bushes, in a long incline of thick pasture. The view from the front porch is perhaps ten miles of unobstructed pastures, hillsides, and greenery. Against the distant, rounded mountainside are farm buildings that look like children's toys. It is breathtaking and arguably one of the most relaxing views in that part of the state. It was the perfect place for Diana to unwind after a day of classes and work, the perfect place to stare out across the deep divide between the tall hillside she lived on and the next promontory.

So far away from the world and yet so close, Morrill is little more than hillside tobacco patches and wild woods. The road running through it is dotted with tiny Breeko block Holiness churches, three small groceries, and a gas pump. It is only five miles from the heart of Berea, but the last mile of the road to Morrill is shielded from the sun and sky on one side by sheer mountain bluff and on the other by tall ancient trees whose branches jut out like an umbrella over the pavement. Driving through it is like passing into an enchanted forest. Its cultivated isolation was the place where the fun of family singing would show the earliest signs of serious promise.

"We'd sit on the porch and sing in the summer, and we'd sit around the fire and sing in the winter," Naomi said about their lives those two years. "Some Sundays we'd sing at the little one-room, all-denomination church there in Morrill, where everyone would jump up and holler and testify and speak in tongues; and where there was a hand-painted wooden sign over the door that said, 'Jesus died for your sins; what have you done for him lately?' "

She found a job working as a midwife for a country doctor, and friends from Morrill remember that she worked for a time in a clinical lab at the EKU teaching hospital. She didn't have to do much work because she didn't need much money to get by in Morrill. Some property owners in the rugged hill country even let members of the gathering group of unrelated dropouts live free in cabins and tiny farm houses just to have them occupied, to keep the woods and weeds from taking them. Margaret Allen had taken a liking to Diana and her children, so their rent for the house was more than reasonable. The child-support check certainly went further up there. Compared to the cost of living (even poorly) in Hollywood, a decent life in Morrill, Kentucky, was a bargain.

Diana enjoyed the company of Morrill residents and a few Berea friends among the teaching and crafts community there. She was outgoing and friendly, quick to share a laugh, and usually bringing a smile to people she met. One local who remembers Diana especially fondly is Robert Chasteen. He is retired now and in his seventies, but he was the handyman around Mrs. Allen's estate when Diana and family lived there.

A twenty-four-year resident of Morrill, Chasteen is something of an amateur historian of the tiny hilltop community. His house is right on the main road through Morrill, and he regularly weeds around the marker plaque he petitioned the state to erect in front of his picket fence. It commemorates the only piece of real history to have occurred there: an early Civil War skirmish that he says ran through his front yard. He is a gentle man who wears a cross outside his work shirt and a baseball cap imprinted with the legend The Gospel Troops. Like a lot of permanent residents of Morrill, Robert Chasteen remembers Diana Ciminella and her family.

"I used to go and have a cup of coffee with them in their kitchen there, and she'd say, 'I don't know what kind of future my little girls are going to have, I want so much for them,' " Chasteen recalled, wiping sweat from his brow with a handkerchief as he rested in the shade in his front yard.

"She used to come see my son David some, and her and the girls would come up to his house up on the hill behind here and sometimes they'd sing while they were visiting David," he continued.

"And she was a Christian!" he explained. It is something he doesn't waste much time ascertaining about people. "She wanted to raise her little girls right. She wanted her little girls to be somebody and to do something. She was strict with them. But Diana was humble and talked with love for everyone. She'd make you love her."

Diana had a very winning personality. Free from the harassments of Hollywood, fixed in a place where she got only as much exposure to the world as she chose to leave the top of Bighill to get, she was once again happy. Smart, good looking, outgoing, and fun to be around, Diana was present-

ing a mighty big standard by which eleven-year-old Christina
was to feel herself measured.

As Robert Chasteen observed, returning to Kentucky
and finding peace at her retreat at Chanticleer renewed
Diana's appreciation of her religious heritage. She began to
take her kids with her to the different little one-room
churches in the area. At one of them—The Miracle Revival
Church of God, Chasteen recalled—Christina and Diana first
began presenting themselves in duets. Sometimes they sang
a hymn Diana remembered from her Ashland Baptist childhood, and other times they joined in with the unrestrained
praise-singing musical styles that have earned Pentecostals
the tag Holy Rollers. Diana didn't seem particular about the
dogmas of these little congregations; it was the pure and
simple act of praising the Creator and raising a little joyful
noise that she wanted to expose her kids to.

"Nobody knows the denomination of the church,"
Naomi recalled. "It was just a southern singin' church."

In addition to fitting into the indigenous community,
Diana's adventurous nature began to find her a place among
the others whose search for solitude and retreat from the
world had led them to the top of Bighill. A practicing vegetarian by the time she got there, she loved learning folk skills
from *Mother Earth News* and *Foxfire*. She took up making lye
soap as a part-time cottage craft and tried with little success
to market the results. Christina was old enough to try her
hand at a traditional Appalachian skill as well.

"Going back to Kentucky I learned where things came
from," Wynonna said. "You couldn't just go down to the store
and get things. We had a garden, and I learned to weave on a
neighbor's loom."

Diana found friends and lovers among the other loners
up on Bighill.

"She got to know a lot of people around this area, 'cause

back then there were a lot of people that had more or less dropped out or at least kicked back a little bit from things, living up in that area," Craig Williams said. "Back then there was a bunch of people, maybe twenty or thirty . . . living in a ten mile radius up there . . . in the woods and different things like that."

She found city people attempting subsistence farming, former musicians trying to find themselves after too many acid trips, and more than a few solitary Vietnam veterans who needed, more than anything, a place to sit and stare and do nothing while their minds adjusted to the brutal futility of their experience now that the war was over. Some of the veterans were darkly brooding men, half spooky from crazy jungle warfare in which no one could safely be assumed to be "on their side." In midseventies language, people who seemed to be wrestling with their own souls for their sanity were called "heavy." Craig Williams was "heavy" in 1974. He lived in a cabin deep in the woods of Morrill.

"Diana . . . was doing exactly what I was doing," Williams recalled. "I was still in a relatively antisocial frame of mind.

"She was overreacting just like I was, just like a lot of people were during that time," Williams said. "The Vietnam War was behind us, but everybody was asking themselves socially what was going on. She was doing the same thing. She wasn't the Lone Ranger by any means by doing that. There were a whole bunch of people up there doing the same thing. Gradually people have remeshed with the society; that's why there are not so many people up there now."

Their many months in Morrill were not as deprived as they sometimes sound. Diana denied herself and her girls modern conveniences for a purpose. She chose to live in what she called genteel poverty and found the simplicity of the isolation stimulating to her imagination, which must have been just a little dulled by the constant sensory overload of the streets of Hollywood. She was resting up for the dreaming of big dreams.

"We lived in a house with no television, no telephone, and no newspaper," Naomi said. "We just had our radio, and on Saturday nights we'd do the wash in our old Maytag wringer washer and listen to the 'Grand Ole Opry.'"

All the culture, fast food, and entertainment she could possibly want was only five miles away in Berea. But up on that big hillside, Diana had the world right where she wanted it. When she wanted to be part of it she got in her car and drove down the hill. Otherwise, she couldn't be reached by anyone or anything that she didn't want to be reached by.

"She put herself in a position where she was incommunicado with the world, except for what she herself dictated," Craig Williams explained. "She went out to the world and picked and chose what she was going to do. She needed that space; she needed that time to get herself focused back in on what she was about."

Diana wanted Christina and Ashley to mesh with their heritage, as she defined it, for at that time the girls considered after-school soap operas and reruns of old situation comedies to be integral parts of their true heritage. In California, they had, in essence, become Hollywood couch potatoes. For every convenience of modern technological life she took away from their new environment, Diana gave them back activities of cultural discovery like baking bread and hand washing laundry. For good measure she added elements of romanticized Appalachian culture to enrich the experience for them.

"I wanted them to see a vanishing way of life," Naomi explained. "When you don't have all that stimulation you resort to your own creativity."

Of course, the first thing one is likely to experience when

"all that stimulation" is removed is a profound sense of tedium.

"You can imagine: here was this kid who had been used to watching TV and having everything," Wynonna said. "I didn't have to look for fun [in California]; it all was there; never a dull moment."

Ashley was still young enough to transfer her attention to her dolls when they got home from school in Berea, but Christina was especially unimpressed with life sans television. Life in Morrill didn't offer as much outside stimulation in a week as Hollywood did in an hour. She was bored and confused about why they were there.

"Christina had a good sense of humor, and she was pretty assertive, you know," said Craig Williams. "I could tell she wondered what the hell they were doing up on that mountain. . . . Part of the problem they had was that Christina felt like she was being isolated for no apparent reason."

The isolation of Chanticleer threw the two children at each other for companionship in a manner more intense than most siblings.

"It did a lot for me," Wynonna said. "It forced my sister Ashley and me to learn to get along and be each other's best friend. When you're a child, you just take things like that for granted. She made us live without TV, which forced Ashley and me to play together and learn to love each other. So many kids end up not having anything in common with their brothers and sisters, and I think that's real sad. In retrospect, the things that Mom forced us to do are just wonderful."

Only boring people stay bored for long, and Christina was too compulsive for that. She made a playmate of a Bighill girl whose interests included music.

"I ran with a girl named Ramona Van Winkle who played guitar and sang [in church]," Wynonna explained. "I had a guitar given to me, and I started banging around on it. I had to teach myself. Nobody was around for lessons."

It was the first small step on the road to the Judds.

"If it wasn't for Morrill, we wouldn't be here today," Wynonna confirmed. "Mom did it, I guess, to save us. That's where I discovered music. I think because of the fact that we didn't have a telephone, we didn't have television, I had to resort to different kinds of entertainment. It forced me to be creative. It forced me to form my own ideas rather than just watch TV and waste my imagination."

Christina's conversion from bored preteen to driven music student didn't occur until the warm weather was gone and cabin fever set in at Chanticleer. Diana originally suggested music as a diversion.

"It was fine in the summertime, but during the first long winter we had to have some kind of home entertainment," Naomi has said. "Someone had given Wynonna a funky old guitar and taught her a couple of chords, so we decided to make our entertainment with that."

Christina had suddenly found something to fill the emptiness. The time on the big hill fired her musical imagination in a way that had once been hinted at when her father gave her a toy tape recorder for Christmas one year.

"I gave her a recorder as a stocking filler, and two days later she was playing along with the songs," recalled Mike Ciminella. "She could sit at the piano and pick things out."

Diana encouraged Christina to learn an instrument. Her first musical instrument had been a plastic guitar that she had gotten as a present when she was three years old. That was now replaced by a real one. It wasn't an expensive one; Diana's budget wouldn't have stretched as far as a good Martin or Gibson. But the new guitar was good enough for Christina to be able to get her fingers around the neck, and when she worked diligently at learning a new chord, it would ring out clearly.

As soon as Christina learned a few tunes on her guitar, she began hauling it around Morrill. One place she often wound up at was Jack Sparks's grocery store. Sparks Grocery is an old white clapboard store with the meat counter and fresh-fruit bin in the back by the wood stove. When you come through the old screen door, stepping onto ancient oiled wood floors, you are also entering the unofficial civic center of the sleepy little community. Jack and Mary Sparks live in the small house that connects through an open doorway behind the cash register. With friends and neighbors dropping by for a loaf of bread and their mail at intervals during the day and early evening, the store seems to serve as much as the Sparks's living room as a retail grocer.

"Christina was just a little thing then," Jack Sparks said, leaning against the old mechanical register. "She used to ride her bike down here and haul that guitar around."

Even then the younger Judd liked an audience. Jack Sparks pointed toward the meat counter where a pair of ladder-back chairs are placed with comfortably worn cushions in the seats.

"She would sit right over there and beat on it," he drawled.

Mary Sparks remembered the pretty young mother better.

"Diana, sometimes she'd come sit around and talk," Mary recalled. "She was a real nice turned person. You never heard no complaint."

She paused to consider the Judds' grocery etiquette. She probably keeps the store's current accounts in her head and hasn't let a deadbeat slip from her memory since the day she and Jack acquired the place.

"No, I don't believe she ever asked for credit, leastwise not here. She always paid for what she got."

In the hard-scrabble world of mountain-top Kentucky backwoods, that alone tells a lot about a person's circumstances and character. Diana Ciminella was an independent straight shooter.

Childhood piano lessons and Diana's family sing-alongs of past years bear little relation to the development of Diana and Christina Ciminella into Naomi and Wynonna Judd. Morrill, Kentucky, was the beginning of that future. Diana seemed to sense early that her daughter's voice at age eleven was already coming on strong. It was still a child's voice, but far better than average, and with the right encouragement and discipline, who knew what might happen? Diana wanted the best for her daughters and she wanted more from life for herself. With no definitive indication that this was the ticket out of the crowd for them, Diana began to push Christina just to see what she was capable of.

"She picked up on it pretty easily," said Craig Williams, who probably has the most valid claim among the handful of Berea-area residents who profess responsibility for teaching the future Wynonna Judd her first song. No other man was as close to Diana during that period. He shared a lot of family time with them. "I think I might have been playing in a band right around that time. I know we spent a lot of time either on their back porch or [with] them out at my cabin.

"When they'd come visiting, almost the first thing that'd happen would be the guitars would come out. We'd start singing and Diana would play percussion on the table top or something and sing along. Christina would try to follow on the chords. You know, after a while we'd play through a song two or three times; then we'd start to get loud on it, you know. That's when you got your confidence built up."

As Williams remembered, it was a Charlie Daniels song,

"Long-Haired Country Boy," that Christina first mastered at his rustic country cabin. "C–G–F; I was a killer on those three-chord songs," he said.

"For the first few months all we knew were songs in the key of C," Naomi explained. "We never had any lessons of any kind because I just never had the money. I used to feel real guilty about it."

The traditional country number "The Sweetest Gift (A Mother's Smile)" has been designated "officially" as the first joining of harmonies by the budding Judds. The song, which is regularly used in the Judds' repertoire in concerts today, originated in 1949 by the duo of brothers Bill and Earl Bolick, who performed as the Blue Sky Boys. The song received wide reissue in the midseventies, including covers by Linda Ronstadt, Emmylou Harris, and Hazel Dickens and Alice Gerrard, who were a popular traditionalist duo recording for Rounder Records in the midseventies. And that's where the Judds picked it up.

"We learned it from Hazel and Alice," Naomi said.

"That was the first song we sang for RCA when we auditioned," Wynonna recalled.

The song served a purpose closer to home when they first learned it. Diana used it to touch the emotions of her mother, who had been a little disappointed that her girls hadn't come all the way home to Ashland to live.

"We learned that song to give to my mother for a Mother's Day present," Naomi said. "We were too poor to buy her a present. . . . So we learned this song off an old Appalachian duet called Hazel and Alice that I found on Rounder Records in a discount bin. I fell in love with the song."

Hazel and Alice were not so old, though their style was. Contemporary folkies, they were just one of several traditionalist acts whose records Diana was bringing home to Chanticleer from bargain bins in second-hand record stores and K-marts to bolster the Appalachian atmosphere of their home. Friends from the Berea College music department took an interest in exposing the children to the music of the Kentucky hills, also. Christina found her ears opening to music for the first time.

"I discovered music, that's the key word," she said. "Until I was about twelve years old, I was a typical kid; I didn't spend money on music. I didn't until we moved to Kentucky and started attending bluegrass festivals."

Once Christina became hooked on music, there was little her mother could do to keep her from buying albums—and little she could say to get the child to do anything else.

"The music was the problem sometimes," Naomi recalled. "Wynonna would take the last few dollars out of the sugar jar to buy guitar strings. I couldn't get her to do her chores, and she used to shove all the dirty dishes under the bed."

"The neurotic, dramatic Naomi Judd of life," Wynonna has termed her mother on days when they aren't getting along, and her mother was a little of both in the child-rearing portion of her Morrill experience. Diana prized her privacy. Few people in Morrill got close enough to see that strain in the family, which often closed up into a tight family circle for healing doses of family closeness for days at a time. In retrospect, Wynonna recalls the period with special fondness.

"I think if you asked me what my favorite time in my life has been, it would be then, now that I look back," she said. "The school system wasn't great. They spend more money on roads in Kentucky than they do [on] the schools, so school bored me a little bit and my studies started going downhill a little because I lost interest. But I became creative."

Christina, nearing puberty, was beginning to assert herself as a person—a fancy way of saying that she turned rebellious. One way that she achieved her own identity was by excessive binging on candy bars and junk food. She had always been a husky child, but she added a couple of extra layers of cellulite to her natural baby fat—a constant bone of contention between mother and daughter. Diana overreacted to this and for a long time continued to dress Christina "like a fat girl" in outfits that were supposed to hide, but actually exaggerated, her size.

Christina and her mother began having some serious clashes while they lived on Bighill. Diana was a very strict mother with her girls, stricter than most parents, from all descriptions. Having come to this place of rest and reorientation after what she would term a fairly wasted youth from seventeen to twenty-five, she was determined that her girls would do better. In an attempt to lay the groundwork for their adulthood, she applied her overdramatic style to the task of discipline. Like her own mother, Diana was extremely stubborn. The constant nagging about Christina's weight and her neglect of household chores, as well as the isolation, caused friction between Diana and Christina.

"She was a very good mother, actually," explained Williams. "I think having been recently out of a divorce and all and having the reality of being a single parent, she may have gone a little beyond the normal disciplinary routines that the average person would have adhered to.

"They're both very strong-willed people," he continued. "Diana, being the authority, would exert some of her will. Christina, being the child, and a very strong-spirited one at that, would try to come right back. So things seemed to have an air of mounting on top of each other to see who was going to give first, you know. And Diana got her way, I mean all the time. She never let go. Once she determined that she was going to stick to something, she pretty well did."

Overprotective, overdramatic—even when Diana wasn't in one of the increasingly frequent battles of will with

Christina, there were instances of parental caretaking that illustrate the nature of this mother-daughter relationship. When their first springtime in the pasture and fruit-tree surroundings of the house in Morrill brought alien pollen Christina's way, she had her first allergy attack. Whatever she was allergic to, it closed her throat with swelling and gave her asthmalike symptoms. Diana, who had an almost fetishlike penchant for cleaning, was aghast.

"Jesus and germs are everywhere, girls . . ."

She looked up the girl's symptoms in the Merck Manual, a do-it-yourself reference guide popular with home-cure fanatics. She was giving the idea of becoming a rural physician some thought. It was just another passing fantasy, but her terror at Christina's bad allergic reaction gave her the excuse to try her hand at medicine. Diana began bringing home drugs to which she had access through her nursing work and gave her shots to cure her. After about a week, said Williams, she was made to see reason, and she stopped trying to doctor the girl by herself. The season passed, taking its pollens with it, and the girl got better.

". . . so say your prayers and wash your hands."

F·I·V·E

Mountain Soul Music

Diana baited a lot of hooks when she moved to the country, at least one of which she wasn't aware. She hadn't given up her amorphous ambitions; she was just giving them a rest. There has always been a streak of altruism in Naomi Judd, a desire to help others that was shown in her Good Samaritan aid to Caroline Hovey when she first arrived in Berea. There was an element of the romantic mixed with a desire to be recognized in her motivation to study nursing, about which she said, "[I] wanted to do something to help others and leave my mark in the world."

Nursing was also planned as a reasonable fallback. She needed a career that could guarantee that she'd earn a decent paycheck while she followed her star, so to speak. While she was up on Bighill living out her dreams of regenerative country life, she imagined grander careers.

"I thought about going to med school to become a country doctor," she said. Becoming a physician was never a serious possibility. Still, this woman has never been short of dreams.

Nurse midwifery was a more practical dream, and it had the added advantage of being the latest trend in the holistic medicine movement. Holistic medicine had become a pet interest for her. As with her curiosity about horoscopes, she thought of home cures and holistic medicine as having their roots in "pre-science science." The Eastern Kentucky nursing program was not liberal enough to substantiate her belief in folk medicines with scientific fact. Midwifery combined the healing arts of nurses' training with the attraction of being whole-grain natural.

This passing career thought gives another view of just how easily Diana was swept up in the trends of the day. Midwives had been around since the dawn of time, but when Diana became enamored with the idea in the 1970s, they had suddenly become popular with middle-class women wishing to deliver their baby at home. The nurse-midwife movement called for midwives to have full registered nursing credentials to legitimize their demand for hospital privileges for their practice. It was seen by obstetricians as obvious competition, and in many places they used their influence with hospitals' boards of professional affiliation to exclude nurse-midwives. By the time Diana was ready to leave Morrill it was for her yet a moot point, however. She had not earned enough academic credits from EKU and her earlier UK studies to complete even the associate's degree in nursing, much less the grueling scholastic preparation of premed.

When she originally returned from California, Diana didn't know how long she would actually stay. She expected the slow and steady work toward a nursing degree to be her main catch as she went fishing for careers, but she wasn't able to quit working and buckle down to four straight semesters of full-time studies. Besides, there were plenty of distractions on her rustic mountain top. When Christina took such a sudden and powerful interest in music, it was like watching an unexpected catch start to jiggle the bobber on the pond. Could there be a big one nibbling at the bottom there, or was it just the wind and the waves? Christina's voice was different, much more powerful and evocative than that of a child. Maybe Diana's reaction was intuition, maybe it was just a mother's rosy opinion of her child's abilities, but she thought there was something there—something potentially big, something worth nudging along. Polly thought it was just another of Diana's crazy fantasies.

"I scared my mother to death," Naomi confessed about her decision to concentrate on pushing Wynonna toward becoming a professional singer. "All I had is a belief, a real strong instinct that Wynonna and I had something. I am not a creature of compromise. I never have been. I knew that Wynonna and I had something, but I kept asking myself, 'Is it motherly pride, or does Wynonna really have the kind of voice I think she's got?'"

Musical influences continued to bear on the future Miss Wynonna Judd. Her ears were opened to music like they had never been before. Southern rock, country blues, folk, and traditional country sounds were among the first styles she learned to play and sing. Left to her own devices for entertainment in the house on the hill, the girl became single-minded about her music, seized with it as a full-blown obsession. Although she retained much of her skills from earlier piano lessons, she transferred her wholehearted passion for music into the beat-up old secondhand guitar. Diana sometimes felt guilty because she couldn't afford to give the child formal lessons, but she stubbornly refused to let Christina ask her father for the money.

"I had to teach myself to play and sing," Wynonna recalled. "We couldn't afford lessons, and bluegrass was the first music I heard that had an influence on me.

"All I wanted to do was buy more records and learn

more songs," she explained. "I went to school with kids in the McClain family, and we'd go to bluegrass festivals. I'd think [performing] was real cool. I thought it looked like a great way to have fun. I became so involved and addicted to music that I couldn't see straight. I guess music is really what kept me out of trouble."

Most significant among the Judds' early musical influences were traditional, folk-country, and bluegrass music. Records of these styles were slow sellers and often wound up on special sales tables. They might cost from two to six dollars less than the latest hot popular albums. That being the case, Diana's tight budget matched her "Kentucky heritage" theme. The high whining wails of bluegrass gospel and the unique harmonies of such seminal country acts as the Stanley Brothers, the Louvin Brothers, Rabon and Alton Delmore, and the Carter Family offered sounds that came from the matched vocal chords of a single family.

"From the time I got interested in music, I was really into bluegrass," Wynonna said. "When we lived in Kentucky, we couldn't afford $8.98 albums, so there was a second-hand store near us and we'd go there and buy records for a dollar ninety-nine. They'd turn out to be some of the greatest records in my collection, like the Delmore Brothers, the Boswell Sisters, Hazel and Alice on Rounder, and Ralph Stanley.

"That was the beginning of my musical addiction. At that point in my life, I hadn't discovered Bonnie Raitt or Little Feat. It wasn't until we moved to Marin County [California] that I discovered that kind of music."

At first, the bluegrass bargain records were just part of the fun of playing at being country folk. Diana characterized this period in the upbringing of Christina and Ashley as her crusade to "reeducate them about how cool it is to be hillbilly." But soon the young mother was learning the harmony line to humor and encourage her daughter. Right away, the combination of voices created an impressive sound. Christina was a better singer than her mother, but the sum of their combined voices was even more charged.

The jumping rockabilly styles of Elvis Presley and other early fifties and midfifties country artists turned the youngster on tremendously to the roots that her modern rock records drew from country music. Christina later grew especially fond of Elvis. Her interest in the man and his music would extend far beyond releasing two singles originally recorded by Presley—far, far beyond, to nearly cult fascination.

"I love that old rock 'n' roll, hillbilly rock 'n' roll," Wynonna said enthusiastically. "I love the innocence and the spontaneity; you know, get up there and jam your brains out —vamp 'til you cramp!"

Diana had lugged an inexpensive turntable with her from California. Though it seemed to work right only half the time, it was enough to teach the mother and daughter ways of matching sounds that couldn't be learned in formal music theory books. They learned from commercialized forms of folk sounds that had been combined and perfected over two hundred or more years of rural American culture. Along with wringer washers, lye soap making (Naomi's china doll complexion shows no sign of ever having actually used the abrasive cleanser), and other simple pleasures, traditional country music forms an integral part of the heritage to which Diana exposed her daughters.

This return to Kentucky had been a spiritual healing for Diana. It provided an atmosphere in which she could relax and connect with her family. Diana made the rolling mountain hideaway at Morrill her personal bastion against the disappointments and pressures that she had faced since her split with Ciminella. She went down from the mountain and brought back pieces of the world that she wished to allow into her hermit's dream. Bluegrass and traditional country

Naomi's enthusiasm was impossible to contain after *Had a Dream* became the Judds' first hit record. *(Rick Mansfield)*

Wynonna *(left)* looked so young at her first awards show. She and Reba McEntire watched Statler Brother Don Reid get his television makeup done. *(Alan Mayor)*

Wynonna and her teenage sweetheart Steve McCord enjoyed attending local barn dances around Franklin. *(Alan Mayor)*

Critics have said of the Judds' voices that Naomi is the smoke and Wynonna is the fire. *(Melodie Gimple)*

Comedians Richard Bowden and Sandy Pinkard had a big hit as Wyoming and Nairobi: The Dudds. *(Dean Dixon. © 1984 Warner Bros. Records)*

"Here's to success," toasts Naomi with Brent Maher. *(Melodie Gimple)*

Celebrating the success of the album *Why Not Me* with the Judds are *(left to right)* Woody Bowles, Ken Stilts, RCA Nashville senior vice-president and general manager Joe Galante, Brent Maher, Don Potter, and RCA executive Tim McFadden *(Melodie Gimple)*

The Judds add their gold and platinum records to the walls of RCA's Nashville office along side those of Waylon Jennings and Elvis Presley. (*Melodie Gimple*)

records found their way into the growing repertoire that she sang with Christina.

At a time when Christina and her mother were just starting to match wills against each other in stubborn contests, the music also offered them a means of communicating and cooperating with each other. Although they butted heads more frequently and violently as Christina got older and more independent, her rebellion against her mother was tempered somewhat by their singing together. They might argue about the piles of dirty clothes in the corner of Christina's room or the candy-bar wrappers tossed under her bed, but the desire to hear their mutual harmonies forced them to sit down and sing together even when they might not want to talk to each other. Music became a bridge across the generation gap.

"We started doing it together just to entertain ourselves, with no other recreational outlets," said Naomi. "[After work I was] bone tired, but if I came in and she was at the kitchen table playing and singing, I would forget everything else and we would sing. It started snowballing on us, and we couldn't put it down."

In fact, Christina wouldn't put it down. Diana saw real talent in her daughter, but she also saw the lazy side of the child as well. Christina's voice was more soulful and powerful than that of most children her age. It was apparent that even without the discipline to polish her voice, the child might develop into a good enough singer to get by on the local nightclub circuit. But Diana remembered "Little" Brenda Lee. Having had suitable training and parental direction, Brenda became an international rock 'n' roll sensation before she reached her teens. Soon Diana began insisting in innumerable little ways that Christina perfect what she was doing.

"She just had that air of determination about her and a

desire, a very strong desire, for her daughter to succeed or
even to overachieve perhaps," Craig Williams recalled. In
light of the Judds' subsequent success, he could see Diana's
early encouragement of Christina's musical interests as the
first steps in the mother's direction of her daughter's career.
It was motivated not so much by any conscious realization
that Christina's talent would lead to a career as by Diana's
own need to control and dominate. In this one case, at least,
the child did not resent her mother's pushing. Christina had
the desire, but she needed someone to guide her. Within a
couple of short years the musical interest became a force
unto itself. It was the beginning of a natural symbiotic pair-
ing: Diana's deep but aimless ambition hitched to her daughter's developing talent and magnificent but rudderless obsession with music.

As for the development of a duo style, that came quite
unconsciously. It was dictated as much by the unequal quality of their separate voices as by their early influences. Christina's voice was simply stronger and better than her mother's, so she took the lead.

"Mama's voice is naturally lower than mine," Wynonna
explained, "so she'd sing harmony."

The early development of their overall "sound" was an
organic maximizing of both their natural vocal gifts, but Diana's insistence on perfection was crucial. Once her daughter's gift was discovered, Diana corralled, encouraged, and
did everything she could to put opportunity and influences in
her daughter's path. With a self-proclaimed "maternal instinct like a mountain lion's," Diana also saw the realization
of her own dreams of making a mark in the world as tied to
her daughter's developing talent.

"Our music has just evolved naturally from the very
beginning," Naomi said. "We never did make a conscious
decision to sit down and start singing together. Each and

every step on this journey since then has been spontaneous and natural."

Being duly humble, Naomi gives herself far less credit than she actually deserves.

"I think she groomed Christina to do that," said Craig Williams. "Once she saw what was happening— . . . saw how quickly Christina was picking up on things and that she had a voice—maybe she didn't have . . . the whole thing in focus when she left here, but in the back of her mind she realized that there was something going on there that could click and that she wasn't going to find it up there. I knew how determined she was as a person. She's slick. Now that I think about it, once she saw there was talent there, she really did try to nurture that as Christina began to show the interest."

Diana pushed Christina to achieve her full potential, but it was a direction that her daughter was more than willing to take. At the same time, Diana pushed little Ashley away when necessary to concentrate on the older girl.

"[Ashley would] get a little jealous sometimes when we'd be singing and she'd try to join in, and it was pretty rough sometimes," Williams said.

Naomi has often said that Ashley, as a singer, "couldn't carry a tune in a bucket." They sometimes make a play on words, calling her "the unsung Judd." Ashley became jealous of the attention and extra time given by her mother to her older sister. Unable to participate in their serious singing, she was at first resentful that she had to wait while her older sister's talents were served.

"[Diana would] be telling Christina 'Now do it right,' and Ashley would try to come in there and it would throw the whole thing," said Williams. "Diana would say 'I don't want you doing it right now,' and Ashley would get a little pissed off."

If Ashley couldn't sing on key, she could make other

noise to vie for her mother's attention. Naomi still frets at times, knowing that she paid more attention to the talent of her eldest daughter. Ashley often felt that she had to do something to wedge herself into the close musical communication developing between her mother and her older sister. Naomi remembers those attempts well.

"Wynonna and I would be practicing together, and Ashley would start banging pots and pans to get attention," she said.

Diana did what she had to do to mollify her youngest, but she kept working with Christina, encouraging and rehearsing her. Christina was a willing student, for though she lacked self-discipline, she could really focus on the music. The girl began to understand the special link that music was forming between her and her mother. She used it to heal rifts. Somedays, after they had butted heads in a battle of wills—typically over cleaning chores that Christina put off to daydream or practice her guitar—the girl would purposely station herself in the kitchen, playing and singing a song so that her mother could join in when she got home. Music from those early days was emerging as a healing balm between them. After a while, they both used it to pull themselves closer while other aspects of their personalities pushed them apart in ferocious battles.

Ashley came to recognize that when her mother and big sister were singing, they weren't fighting. Sometimes it seemed to be the only time they really communicated anything but angry competition of wills. This recognition reduced her jealousy of their exclusive collaboration.

Morrill, as a two-year immersion in "country" culture, was a raving success for Diana. When she arrived, there was a certain amount of confusion inside her about whether Kentucky would really be everything she remembered and hoped it would be. In many ways, it was. But after so many years in Los Angeles, wishing to appear sophisticated but clinging to her small town Baptist views, she was still something of a tourist in her own home state. The jaunts to the Pentecostal churches up in the hills around Berea were like taking in local color, an opportunity to practice the beautiful harmonies of traditional country hymns on an appreciative audience. Friends among the Bighill dropouts tagged Diana with the nickname Hollywood because even in her granny dresses and earth shoes, she was the most glamorous and worldly woman up there.

Still, when her rustic return was drawing to an end in late 1976, Diana had taken some lessons to heart about the eastern Kentucky middle-class world. In two years of holding the rest of the world at bay she learned that though she could recover her equilibrium in the woods of Kentucky, she could not thrive there.

"I think she got to recognize that simplicity was not necessarily a negative thing: it can be cool to be a little bit laid back," said Craig Williams, sipping the dregs of a beer as the late afternoon sunlight filtered through the windows of his cabinetry shop.

"Of course, that didn't ever stop her determination, but I think it allowed her to see that it's okay to only go so far for other people and maybe even for herself," Williams continued. "I think it really did her a lot of good, that period of her life. A lot of times I could tell that there was a certain kind of contentment about her just from being around people like Robert Chasteen and stuff."

Another key to her eventual disaffection with Morrill was the continuing development of Christina's musical interest. It blossomed almost daily as she learned new songs and found new strength and nuance in her young-teenager's voice. For that talent to develop properly, it would need exposure to real musicians, and they'd have to go elsewhere for that. Diana's ambitions for herself and for her children were a driving force that could have pulled a coal train across the Great Plains.

One might wonder why, if Diana was so sure that Christina had genuine talent, she didn't just pack up and head to Nashville right then. Country music was growing in popularity by leaps and bounds in the late seventies, and the styles of music acceptable to its fans were becoming broader. Brenda Lee recorded her first pop hit with Nashville's Owen Bradley when she was just twelve. Tanya Tucker had her first huge country hit, "Delta Dawn," at the tender age of fourteen. But Diana considered Christina at thirteen going on fourteen to be too young and unpolished yet. She had a sharp eye to what it would take for the child to have a real shot, and she knew that her time had not yet arrived.

California had long been pulling Diana back. By that time, her best friend from high school was living in San Francisco. Her sister Margaret had also become a California resident. When Diana went to visit a friend in the San Francisco area, she came back enthralled with the beauty of Marin County to the north. California was a long way from home and family in Ashland, which apparently was part of its renewed appeal. Ex-husband Mike Ciminella had moved back to Lexington at about the same time that she'd come back to her home state. It was his best opportunity since his divorce from Diana to interact with his daughters, and he took advantage of it. Diana tried her best to accommodate her daughters' desire to see their father, but she and Ciminella didn't get along well at all. Christina, on the other hand, delighted at seeing her father more regularly.

"He taught me to drive when I was eleven," Wynonna explained. "He said 'Go for it,' while Mother was saying 'Be a nice, sweet little kid.' He's very lighthearted. We can get serious when we need to get serious, but he'd rather drive eighty miles per hour and listen to rock 'n' roll."

During that period, Mike Ciminella introduced his singing daughter to her first major rock concert when the Who played Rupp Arena in Lexington. Christina had inherited her father's Mediterranean emotional makeup. Regardless of Naomi's later assertions that manager Ken Stilts was "the only father figure the girls ever had," Mike Ciminella was involved with his daughters Ashley and Christina (he never uses her stage name Wynonna in references to his oldest child). He was there in spirit or on the phone even when Diana's moves and the circumstances of the Judds' success prevented him from physically being present. He would be Christina's safe haven.

"Daddy is a real rebel," said Wynonna. "He's Italian, and he believes in living dangerously. He's very unlike Mother. It's been a real challenge to me to tell him he's important to me. He's the person I call if I'm unhappy, but he's not there for my birthday. It's been hard.

"It was an emotional tragedy for me when my parents divorced," she explained. "That's when I discovered music. I needed something for *me*, something to escape to."

His proximity and relationship with his daughters may have figured into her return to Kentucky in the first place, and just as likely added to Diana's reasons for fleeing to the West Coast. Diana had to admit that he had become quite successful since their breakup, whereas she had not as yet found her niche. Less than an hour's drive away from Berea in Lexington, he was as close as he'd be again to either child for several years to come.

Her past began pressing relentlessly on Diana as she prepared to leave the mountain top to seek her future. The final motivation to leave was the impending divorce of her parents. Glen's drinking had continued, and the couple's alienation had grown until he finally left home and took up with a much younger woman. For the surviving Judd siblings, that divorce was going to be a nasty one.

S·I·X
California Dreaming

Having disapproved of her daughter's earlier divorce, she now had to face up to her own. Polly Judd decided that her best line of attack in the divorce proceedings would be to call in Diana, Margaret, and Mark to testify in court about their father's drinking and other unfamily-like behavior. She had invested her whole life in the Baptist Church nursery and in raising her family. There seemed little else to show for it but her collection of antique furniture and the lives of her surviving children.

There was little doubt that the court would give her the house, but she wanted more. This was personal. She wanted to alienate Glen from her children's affections by dragging them in as character witnesses against him. There was more venom circulating within the Judd family from the impending divorce of the parents than a basket load of diamondback rattlers could have injected. Built up over the years of drinking, abandonment, and the deep unhealed wounds arising out of Brian's long death by cancer, Polly's anger and sense of survival would backfire with Diana. Forced to choose between her parents, Diana simply opted out. She was secretly pleased with herself for asserting her own emotional needs over those of her mother, even if she hadn't the nerve to do it face-to-face. It was better to keep her memories than betray them, which would have been the price of accommodating Polly's vindictive scheme. But Diana's option had its cost as well. Polly and Diana stopped talking.

Unfortunately, Diana took away little emotional reinforcement from her father to replace what she had forfeited by crossing Polly. Glen Judd had never been able to actively encourage the love of his children. It just wasn't in him. He was not a man given to overt displays of affection. The service station required long hours of exhausting labor—one reason he kept his off-hours at home during the children's younger years was that he was usually too bone-tired from work to go out.

Glen could not give Diana and her siblings the simple satisfaction of telling them he loved them. They had always had to assume that from the fact that he took care of them, provided for them, and showed such small signs of affection as his personality would allow.

But in the autumn of 1976, for all the bitter fruits of losing their parents' union, the adult children of Polly and Glen Judd were chagrined at their mother's demands that they appear in court to repudiate their father. For Diana Ciminella, already planning a change, already poised to once again put behind her the lonely beauty of eastern Kentucky for the coast of California and dreams of a new life, the court date loomed.

The last time that Diana had talked to her mother about testifying, she had just said, "Sure, Mom"—anything to avoid an argument. Having already made her peace with Morrill, she packed everything she owned into a rented truck the night before she was supposed to make her appearance in court and lit out before dawn.

"I could not psychologically face my parents' divorce," Naomi said. "I knew both sides of the story, and my heart was absolutely ripped in two . . . Divorce is one of the roughest things a child can go through; I know, I put my own kids through it. I literally packed up in the middle of the night and moved."

She was prompted by an abiding inner need that she had grown better able to meet in the years since her divorce. Diana needed always to be in control of her situation, even to the point of causing herself additional problems. She'd rather be in charge of her own loss than let someone else dictate the terms of her comfort.

Once she had made up her mind to make a sharp, clean break, she wasted no time doing so. She walked into Craig Williams's cabin one evening and calmly told him that their relationship wasn't what she needed, and it ended right there. Williams had been good to her daughters, encouraging Christina's musical interests and treating them more like individuals with a right to their own minds and wills than Diana was often able to do. But he had been too laid back, unwilling to be accelerated into the world that now beckoned to her with opportunity again. His ambitions were to continue cooling out on the hillside, but Diana's were now focused on getting back into the mainstream, where she and her daughters would have a better chance at excelling.

Besides, she didn't want to take a man along, anyway. She had suffered through the hard lessons of her father's withheld affections and the bitterness that pervaded her post-divorce dealings with Michael Ciminella. For good reasons, she didn't have a lot of faith in her own ability to pick men. She believed in one-man–one-woman relationships but found that permanence was the missing link.

There were things from which she was fleeing, but she was also moving unstoppably toward her own vague ambitions: "the dream" as Wynonna would come to characterize her mother's drive to reach the spotlight. That dream, that sense of being special, if yet unrecognized and unfulfilled, sent her sailing off that hillside like a strong westerly wind. It was time to go, even if it meant losing ground again in her two-college attempt to pile up the sixty to sixty-four credits needed for an associate's degree so she could apply for her RN license. She intended to stay at her next destination long enough to earn her nursing degree, but beyond that—who knew? Wynonna has off-handedly suggested that their second move to California was intended to be a short-lived break rather than a settled couple of years.

"[Mom] went to visit her best friend and fell in love," Wynonna said. "She's a gypsy of the universe. She's not afraid to take a chance."

Naomi Judd still has gypsy stirrings, which helps explain the stimulation she finds in their constant concert touring.

Diana had a support system of people who cared about her back in California. Her dreams were bigger than the whole state of Kentucky could support, and as she had earlier felt when she married Ciminella, she could feel the pressure of other people's dreams impinging on her. The period of cultural reawakening in her children had been accomplished in two years. They all needed exposure to new people once more, to places and educational systems that would broaden their horizons. Regarding her own education, Diana also looked forward to California's sympathy for her synthesis of folk medicine and science.

"If I hadn't been at the head of my class, I might have got kicked out of nursing school in Kentucky for my ideas," she explained. "I wanted to find out the scientific rationale for all the folk medicines I grew up with. When I moved out there I could learn about biofeedback and holistic medicine."

The Judd parents' divorce was finalized just three weeks prior to Christmas in 1976, by which time Diana was long gone. Polly had no formal job training, just those domestic talents that make a family home. She got the house, but for her to prosper and not have to sell it, she would have to assess her strengths. Margaret was married and moved away, Mark was preparing himself for the seminary, and Diana had just disappeared altogether. She could expect no financial help from them. She'd have to work. There was no carefree Christmas in Ashland that year.

As Polly passed through the holidays, she took stock of herself. No matter how she added it up, she still came out with the same verdict: she was a cook and a housekeeper. Neither of those jobs pay much above minimum wage in the general market, but she lived on the Ohio River. By putting herself in a barge kitchen as food manager and chef, she could earn good money. Her work schedule would keep her on the boat three weeks and home three weeks. Gambling and drinking were forbidden on board, so riverboat crews had almost nothing to do when their shift was over but hang out in the galley to play poker for matchsticks and eat. They liked good solid home-style food and plenty of it. She had found her niche.

Polly felt deeply betrayed by Diana's disappearance and refusal to back her in the rancorous divorce suit. She and Diana had little, if any, communication during the next several years, during which Polly fell in love with and married riverboat captain Wib Rideout. Polly's steps toward independence were updated for Diana in letters and phone calls from Mark and Margaret. Diana followed her mother's progress with a combination of pride and nostalgia for the simple

existence she selectively remembered her childhood as being.

Naomi observed, "If anyone knows her way around a
kitchen, [Mama] does. She's my favorite cook in the whole
world. Every time I go to Mama's I know I can find her potato
salad in a green bowl on the second shelf of the refrigerator."

It would be years before she tasted Polly's potato salad
again. She was gone from Kentucky, severing her ties there
for good for all she knew, but she had done it on her own
terms. That was what was ultimately most important to her.

"Well, we didn't always have the [Judd] family," Wynonna recalled. "If it hadn't been for my [Ciminella] grandparents, I wouldn't have had braces or senior pictures or
gone to the prom. But for a while they thought we were the
weirdest people in the world. They thought Mom was some
creature from outer space because she had this dream."

This move was accomplished, according to Naomi, with
her driving the biggest U-Haul truck she could rent, with her
two daughters sitting on the front seat beside her. California
was as far away as she could get and still be someplace familiar.

On the first day of her second exodus from Kentucky,
Diana drove west on U.S. I-64. The afternoon sun came
through the front windshield of the U-Haul truck cab. As St.
Louis approached, perhaps an hour or two ahead, she
thought maybe there'd be a place to stay overnight on the
Illinois side of the river. It had been a long, lumbering day
pushing the do-it-yourself moving van northward through
Louisville, then on through the landscape of lower Indiana
and Illinois, so similar to that of central Kentucky. No, it was
more important to get across the Mississippi River before
stopping for the night. That would put an important
landmark between her and the troubling family issues she'd

left behind in Ashland. A new and exciting life awaited her in California, still many days' drive away.

Packing up the old U-Haul and pointing it in a new direction every so often was becoming a regular event in their lives, one that gave them a sense of intimacy as each other's only constants. Each move, each new location, enriched their outlook, if not Diana's pocketbook, and offered new insights into the last place they'd been. Money always seemed hard to come by. Diana seemed rarely able to get much of a savings account going, but the girls were getting to see more of the world around them than most children. It gave Christina and Ashley an edge of worldliness to balance against the emotional vulnerability that they had inherited from their mother. Christina, especially, had emotions that kept her moody—up one day, down the next. "She's a real emotional kid," Naomi explained. "*Real* emotional." Ashley had already made peace with being excluded from their music.

Continually having to establish themselves in new places would give them an advantage over other people who grew up and stayed in one place, having only their narrow, parochial experience by which to judge everything else. Besides, Diana thought, it wasn't like they didn't have fun jumping around the country. Once she had seen to her children's needs, she wanted to have fun.

Winter classes at the two-year community college at Kentfield, College of Marin, got started in chilly, clammy weather in early 1977. They were closer to San Quentin prison than to the hilly harbor town of San Francisco. Diana had to drive only about five miles from the tiny village of Lagunitas, where she rented a one-bedroom walk-up apartment, to register for night classes.

Just as in the year that Diana split with Ciminella, there

would be no snow for them that winter; not like the thick blanket of white that gently covered the eastern Kentucky highlands. Northern California temperatures would get down to around forty-five degrees at night; damp and chilly. A deep fog could roll in on mornings when it wasn't actually raining. It rained one day out of three and acted like it wanted to much of the rest of the time.

Diana liked her new school. It found value in her herbal medicines. Founded in 1926 as Marin Junior College, its student body had voted to adopt the less pejorative appellation in 1948. The vast majority of College of Marin's eleven thousand students were boning up on remedial courses in hope of transferring to one of the four-year colleges in the area, but the high number of adults returning to complete their education was reflected in the fact that 25 percent of Marin's classes were scheduled after 5 P.M. The San Francisco–Oakland–Berkeley area is teeming with intellectuals, artists, writers, musicians, and other creative people—a college-town atmosphere that spread north into Marin County. With a U.S. census count of more than fifty thousand college and university students in the area, that part of California has one of the highest concentrations of academics in America.

After taking course work at the University of Kentucky in the midsixties and then piddling through the Eastern Kentucky University program for a year and a half, Naomi would have to buckle down to another year and a half of full-time night-school studies in California to eke out what should have been a two-year associate's degree in sciences.Having cut her ties with Kentucky, this new regimen was particularly hard on her, straining her ability to support herself and the girls. There she was, living in the midst of a very affluent community in less-than-affluent circumstances. But if she couldn't be rich, she could be near people who were. They were so much more interesting.

"Mom's country at heart, but she's been California polished," Wynonna said. "She's seen fast-lane things. That's been a part of our thing, I think."

Not long after they moved back to California, Diana Ciminella decided that she was ready for another major change in her life. She wanted a new name. It was a simple matter of petitioning in Marin County Court to restore her maiden name: Judd. She had kept Ciminella's name only for the convenience of sharing her children's last name. She wanted to shed that constant reminder of her failed marriage now that she was thousands of miles away from her ex-husband again. She decided that Ciminella wasn't even a convenient name. She had always thought Ciminella was "horrendous, so Catholic, so Italian."

"If I called for pizza or went for dry cleaning, they'd put it under S and Z," she explained. "I was having a time with this long name. Whatever I did, it gave me troubles, and I did not feel like a Ciminella. I was a Judd and darned proud of it."

While she was at it, she decided to shed the name Diana, too. She felt at the time that it wasn't close enough to her own spiritual, rural Kentucky conception of her true heritage. A traveler in a foreign culture, Diana looked to the Book of Ruth in her Bible for a name attached to a woman whose story bore not a few similarities to her own. Without trying to press that point too finely, the biblical Naomi followed her husband into a strange land where, at length, she found herself left without her husband or any other male relatives to care for her. Naomi had only a pair of girls, widows of her sons, who were like daughters to her. The choice of Naomi for her new name was prophetic for Diana, for the Bible story tells of the Hebrew woman Naomi continuing her travels in search of a home in her former homeland and eventually leaving one of the daughter figures behind before finding her reward thanks to the other girl.

All that Diana had to do was present proof of her divorce, and the courts would restore her maiden name. There was only one problem: she didn't have any such proof. When she contacted the Los Angeles Superior Court for a copy of her final divorce papers, there simply weren't any. She had never completed the process to get her final decree, thinking that her interlocutory decree was enough. That July, Diana took a short trip south along the California coastline to Los Angeles, where she finished the process of divorcing Michael Ciminella, restoring to herself the name Judd and taking the new name Naomi while she was at it.

Not long after Diana Ciminella legally became Naomi Judd, Christina also became interested in a name change.

"I made my own decision to change from being Christina Ciminella to being Wynonna Judd," Wynonna explained. "Ciminella was so Italian, and it always sounded like that disease salmonella." She decided that as long as her mother was getting a new life in California and a new name, she would do the same.

"The reason I changed it was that when I discovered music, I felt like I took on a whole new identity," Wynonna explained in an insightful interview in the radio trade magazine the *Gavin Report.* "I had found something that changed my life, made me happy and got me through the hard times."

There has been some discussion about whether "Wynonna" is one of the Indian-princess fantasy names Naomi gave herself as a child, or whether it was just an approximation of some of the colorful names she had heard in rural Boyd County. It has even been suggested that the name means "first born" in Seminole Indian language, but the name was actually borrowed from the small southwestern town of Wynona, Oklahoma.

"I got the name from a song called 'Route 66,'" she explained. "There's a line that says, 'Flagstaff, Arizona, don't forget Wynona.' So I just decided to change it. I know people probably think I changed for professional reasons, but that's not why." "Route 66," the popular 1940s song by Nat "King" Cole, was undoubtedly brought to Wynonna's attention in the version of it done by Texas swing band Asleep at the Wheel, which charted at forty-eight in 1976.

Wynonna also adopted her grandmother's name, Ellen, for her new middle name. Naomi tried to get Ashley into the new-name business, suggesting that she become Ramona to match Wynonna. Ashley thought that the names her mother suggested for her were hilarious. If everyone else had a need to create new identities, she didn't. She nixed Ramona but agreed to go by Judd, though to this day she legally remains a Ciminella. Christina began using the name Wynonna and took her mother's maiden name, but she too stopped short of actually making the change permanent at that time.

Needing to work, Naomi started out in Marin's night school. Her course load showed that she had finally gotten serious about earning her degree.

"I'd lay awake at night wondering how I was gonna put food in the kids' bellies the next day," Naomi recalled. "Being a waitress all day and going to nursing school at night, I'd have to go on three or four hours' sleep a night. I just had late afternoon and early evening to cook and do the laundry and supervise the kids' homework and all that."

Naomi determined to buckle down and finally finish her studies, though. She didn't want this trip to California to end up in a frustrating and tiring string of secretarial and semi-professional modeling assignments. No matter that her good looks and friendly personality brought good tips; she had no desire to be a waitress the rest of her life. She was well aware that few old waitresses, stuck refilling coffee cups in truck-stop diners, ever intended to end up there either. That was the road to nowhere, and nowhere was not even an alternative destination on her itinerary anymore. Her dream had no clear detail, but its force could not be denied. Wishing to be finished with school, she shifted her schedule of course work to day school, where she could get more credits in a shorter time. She attended classes all day, Monday, Wednesdays, and Fridays.

"Tuesdays and Thursdays were what they called clinicals, where we actually went into hospitals and practiced what we were learning," Naomi recalled. "I had some pretty heavy-duty days."

There was change, but there was continuity in this move across the continent. Her California friends showed her where the fun was in San Francisco when she wanted stimulation. Her beauty and eager, outgoing personality helped her make friends. People there lived in lavish houses, soaked in hot tubs, and practiced some of the same "all-natural" habits of health and diet that she had found to be necessities back in the genteel poverty of Kentucky. It was an exotic kind of home away from home.

Her earlier trips scouting the area had given her the lay of the land and had revealed her options. Ever the hermit, she preferred to skirt the urban crush of the San Francisco Bay area, opting instead to cross the Golden Gate Bridge and nest in the upscale woodsy reaches of central Marin County past San Rafael. She went about as far into the woods and as close to the preserves of park lands as she could get in choosing the tiny hamlet of Lagunitas. With only fifteen hundred residents, Lagunitas seemed more insulated from the rapid growth swelling the rest of the county, giving Naomi crucial sanctuary when she needed it.

Marin County grew steadily as disaffection grew for the hippie scene born in the Haight-Ashbury district of San Francisco in 1967. People with the means, artistic people like musicians and writers, even the odd laid-back investment banker, flocked northward from Frisco in a constant stream from the late sixties through the early eighties. By the time Naomi and her brood moved there, San Rafael and its suburbs had spread nearly up to Novato and as far out into the hot-tub hinterlands of the county as Lagunitas itself, but there it stopped.

In relative terms, the county sustained one of the highest growth rates of any area in the nation: 120 percent population expansion between 1972 and 1982. Still, there was more than enough room for eccentricity and artistic life-styles. If you have enough money, California has plenty of room for just about anything you have a mind to do. Without money, it takes significantly more imagination.

"One year we lived in a one-bedroom apartment over a real estate office [next to the post office]," Naomi recalled later. "Wynonna slept in the bedroom, and Ashley and I used a mattress in the other room. We went to Fairfax [about 20 miles away] once a week to do the laundry."

Rural Marin County was like an upscale version of Morrill, Kentucky, in many ways. Naomi exaggerates the rurality of her own upbringing for dramatic effect, but she aptly contrasts the elective life-style of wealthy Marin Countians with the necessity of similarly living in Appalachian Kentucky.

"When we came out [to Lagunitas], it was a lot like home," she said. "I was raised on garden veggies, no makeup, bare feet, and midwifery because that's the way of life in the mountains. Out [in California] people were into it by choice."

It paralleled the life-style that she had adopted in Morrill, only on a much more expensive scale. Wynonna made similar observations and comparisons.

"On the one hand, I went to school with Appalachian kids who had never been out of the county," she explained.

"Then I moved out to Marin, where most of my friends' parents were divorced and people were into hot tubs and vitamins. . . .

"When we lived [in Marin County] it was more like a hippie thing. I was like thirteen, and *all* my friends' parents were divorced. If they were married, it was a unique thing. I went to a neat open school that believed in children learning at their own capacity. It's a really weird place, but I'm glad I lived there."

In Marin County Wynonna's interest in music passed the hobby stage. It was hard for Naomi to get the girl to even do her homework after school. All she wanted to do was to play her guitar and sing. There was little time for Ho Ho's and sitcom reruns for her after school. She was strictly a born-again Valley girl with a taste for Lowell George, Joni Mitchell, and Bonnie Raitt records. At thirteen, the blisters that she used to get on the tips of her fingers when she started playing guitar had been replaced with hardened calluses. Wynonna was serious about music, and everything else, from school work to household chores, could take an ol' cold tater and wait.

Wynonna's voice developed fast. Her willingness to practice gave her mother satisfaction, but her stubborn refusal to accept responsibility in the other areas gave discipline-conscious Naomi conniptions. They were hardheaded, each determined to have her own way. They seemed to bring out the best and the worst sides of each other. With genetically complementary voices, they were becoming more closely linked almost by the hour.

"She makes me laugh the hardest and she makes me madder than anyone else on earth," Naomi confessed. She also had a voice that was Naomi's only chance at making a commercially viable commodity of her own.

As music became a more pervasive force in their lives

during this second retreat to California, Naomi and Wynonna emerged as prototypes of their current musical identities as the Judds. Friends from Novato, California, remember that the pair performed locally and in churches as the Judd Sisters, though the girls deny it. They say the only name they ever considered using professionally, besides Naomi and Wynonna Judd, was the Kentucky Sweethearts.

Wynonna worked harder at her music than at anything else in her life, including high school, which she started while in California. It would become apparent from their next move, after Naomi got her degree from College of Marin and began working as a free-lance nurse substituting for vacationing RNs at various hospitals, that Naomi had, by that time, decided that there was real commercial potential in the combination of their voices. Wynonna was thinking of the music for its own sake, however. Naomi had not yet merged her daughter's potential with her own dream.

"We weren't sitting around saying 'We've got to practice today because a year from now we want to go to Nashville,'" she said. "It never occurred to us."

If that obvious eventuality hadn't occurred to her, it seemed to be occurring to just about everybody else who knew them.

"Ashley had one of her friends over, and Mom and I were in the living room singing," Wynonna recalled. "Her little friend said, 'What are they doing?' Ashley said, 'Oh, they think that they're going to be country-music stars.'"

For Naomi, it was a point of pride and a point of entry to the local music scene. She didn't really have personal ambitions as a singer but longed for acceptance among that community of talented players and singers. Naomi made friends among the session players and acoustic newgrass musicians in the area, confidently approaching talents she admired after she and Wynonna had watched them perform in a club or lounge. Among the people she says she got to know at that time are acoustic jazz-bluegrass ensemble leader David Grisman, harmonica player Norton Buffalo, and Emmylou Harris. Emmylou's bandleader at that time was Ricky Skaggs, who had come from Louisa, Kentucky, just a few miles from Ashland. When Naomi heard him tell of his hometown from the stage, she realized that it was the same stretch of countryside where she had spent her own summers with her grandparents. Skaggs instantly liked the brash and beautiful Naomi, who distinguished herself in a club crowd one night by calling out to ask him when he had last eaten at a hometown restaurant only a Boyd County Kentuckian would know. He later helped her make important contacts when she became serious about seeking a career in music.

Once Naomi began earning a nurse's wage, she decided to seek out a professional musician to give lessons to both her girls. She wanted advanced instruction for Wynonna. Ashley got fiddle lessons, but it was tough finding a guitar teacher whose abilities outstripped Wynonna's own. Those who played better than the thirteen-year-old were too much in demand as studio pickers to give lessons.

Peter Adams and Robin Yeager, two musicians then associated with Virgo One Studio in Novato, helped Wynonna get her first experience behind a microphone. Adams met Naomi when she came into the music store where he worked to buy guitar strings. Their friendship grew, and he was invited over to dinner at the cabin Naomi eventually rented on the outskirts of town. There, the mother and daughter played and sang duets around the kitchen table after dishes were cleared. Adams heard only Wynonna's voice as especially strong. He would not be the last to underestimate the contribution of Naomi's contralto harmonies.

"I never thought that Naomi was that good a singer, but

Christina . . . ," Adams said. "When she did things like 'The Midway' [by Joni Mitchell], it just knocked me over."

Adams invited them to Virgo One so that his friend Yeager, who was a local producer, could meet them and hear Wynonna sing. Naomi had low expectations from the meeting but found it exciting to hang around professional musicians and their work places. For Wynonna, the exposure to the studio when she was thirteen helped her make a mature commitment to her music. For the first time, she began thinking of this as a serious course for her life.

"She kind of grew up and decided she really wanted to do this with her mom," said Robin Yeager.

When he set aside some free studio time for Wynonna to try her hand at recording for the first time, it was a pivotal turn for the youngster. The surroundings and trappings of a professional studio intimidated her, but her performance, according to Yeager, was nothing less than dynamic.

Wynonna and Naomi first recorded together at Yeager's Virgo One studios in 1977. That session consisted of four tunes, including the one that Yeager remembers best, "Let Me Be Your Baby." Wynonna took this as a solo vocal, but she couldn't do it without her mother standing by her side in the studio.

"I'll never forget that," Yeager recalled. "She was very much a little girl. We started to get the thing rolling, Naomi was in the control room with us, and Christina said, 'Mama, can I talk to you?' "

The session came to a halt, everyone sitting around the cramped, dimly lit control room trying not to be obvious about watching the petrified youngster seeking encouragement from her mother. The engineer turned off Wynonna's microphone to give them a little privacy. Then Naomi gave the high sign and the tape got rolling again. With her mother at her side, Wynonna cut loose with a rock-tinged country-blues voice stronger and more mature than any thirteen-year-old since Brenda Lee or Tanya Tucker.

Naomi found herself being swept up in her daughter's musical obsession. The Virgo One sessions were just for fun, though they lit a fire under Wynonna. Remembering her own troubles in finishing high school, Naomi would insist that her daughter "keep it at home, around the table" rather than seek bookings as a professional singer until she got out of school. Still, Naomi thrilled at the sound of their voices mingling in the kitchen and sometimes sacrificed to get new material for them to learn.

"I remember I was in a bookstore to buy some medical books—they are so expensive—and I thought, I'm not going to spend $120 on these books," Naomi recalled. "I'm going to Discount Bin and buy some records so we can learn some more songs."

Wynonna was hooked on music, and she knew what she wanted to do with it. Naomi, though convinced that her daughter had talent and further certain that the girl's best sound was in duet with her, had her own agenda to consider.

S·E·V·E·N

Last Stop Before Nashville

Naomi found work closer to the San Francisco area, and it paid well. She saw the worst of her privations in Lagunitas, chopping her own wood in the damp chill of the northern California winter—this time because she *had* to more than wanted to. Moving away from Kentucky this last time had ruffled a lot of family feathers. Polly Judd eventually cooled her anger at her daughter, but the help line was not resurrected. Polly, on her own for the first time in her adult life, was starting to put her own life back together. She had neither the extra cash nor the inclination to send any to a daughter who had not only rejected her plea for testimony but had cast off the name she'd given her thirty-one years earlier.

Though Michael Sr. and Mary Ciminella never ceased their interest in their grandchildren, the girls' father certainly wasn't going to chip in to help support Naomi's latest wild adventure, especially since she took his children out of his reach again. His contribution to the girls' support was likely to have increased, since he was able to have them up for weekends in Lexington. Now Naomi had split for the coast and his daughters were far out of reach. He had found his niche in marketing and advertising in the thoroughbred business, orbiting between Lexington and Ocala, Florida. He wasn't about to chase a gypsy ex-wife all over the nation to keep contact with his two girls. There'd be no end to it. Disgusted with Naomi, he followed his own opportunities and moved to Ocala in 1979.

Naomi burned a lot of bridges when she struck out for the West, but she was on her own, which suited her just fine. Wynonna and Ashley thrived on the semiregular changes of scenery.

Once Naomi had done a few free-lance photo modeling sessions down in San Francisco, taken some temporary nursing assignments at decent pay, and put herself a few dollars ahead, she made a purchase that said more about her sense of style than the need for basic transportation. She bought a car, but not just another clunker capable of pulling a U-Haul trailer. Naomi bought a vintage red and white 1957 Chevy, fully reconditioned, a car that drew stares wherever it went. Naomi liked being the center of attention, and that car put her there even on a trip to the grocery store. One night as she drove around nearby San Raphael, day dreaming and considering adventure, that car paid for itself by attracting a unique opportunity.

The George Lucas film company had just started work in the area on the sequel to the popular movie *American Graffiti.* A search was on for period automobiles to add atmosphere to the film. Someone spotted Naomi and her car, resulting in an offer to rent the car and give the driver a bit part in the film. Naomi bargained to get Wynonna a nonspeaking role as an extra for a couple of crowd scenes, as well —all this because she had felt like getting out that night.

"What I was doing was cruising," she confessed. "The kids were home in bed and I was cruising."

More American Graffiti pitched the main characters of
the original film several years forward into the 1960s, to a
time of campus protests over the Vietnam War. Naomi had
been too busy back in Lexington with her first baby when
such events really happened. Wynonna and Naomi were
among the dozens of extras playing student protesters rally-
ing around student speakers. The script called for them to be
chased by riot police before eventually being captured and
loaded into a prison bus. Naomi ingratiated her way into a
role that eventually got listed in the credits of the film:
Naomi Judd as Girl on Bus. She had hustled one brief line to
deliver in that scene, but it got edited out of the film when it
was sold for television. That was the only point in the film
where she could be clearly recognized. Fickle fame, thou
fleeting candle.

After their scenes were through shooting, Naomi wran-
gled a job as a production secretary on the project. She figured that if she had to drive her car down daily (she had no
other transportation and couldn't simply leave it on the set
for an indefinite time) she might as well hang around and
make herself useful. A woman willing to work hard at carrying scripts and fetching coffee can be quite useful on the set.

When the Lucas company wrapped up their shooting in
the San Francisco area, Naomi found herself with a nice nest
egg left from the car rental. As a swing-shift nurse, working
for temporary agencies to fill in anywhere a hospital might be
shorthanded, she knew she could find good paying work just
about anywhere. She was once again eager to go adventur-
ing.

There are lost weeks and months in the chronology of
Naomi Judd's wanderlust odyssey that include attempts at
living in Chicago, a short experiment in returning to Ashland, and some cold months on the Kentucky River in the
rural outback south of Lexington near Nicholasville. With a

little money, a fully restored '57 Chevy, and a have-U-Haul-will-travel spirit of adventure, the young mother of two was tied to no particular place when there was the hint of something new and exciting somewhere else. She jokes about her own wandering ways.

"I think Wynonna's memories of growing up are hanging out in the back of a car zipping up and down America's highways hollering 'Where are we going and when are we going to get there,' " she said. "And I'm saying, 'I don't know. Just wherever it looks good, I'll stop. We'll live there for a while.' "

Legend holds that Naomi and the girls left California bound for Nashville in May of 1979. Wynonna got her favorite birthday cake—devil's food with chocolate icing—as she turned fifteen on the way to that uncertain destination. She had gotten used to that. Wynonna and Ashley were sick of roadside motel rooms by the time they hit Nashville, but they were in for a stretch at a travel court in an area where rooms at different establishments were rented by the hour or by the week, depending on the customer's needs. Naomi spent most of the money she'd socked away from working on *More American Graffiti*, and she recalled those first couple of weeks in Nashville as "living in a Murfreesboro Road motel and living on crackers and bologna" while she checked around for work and more permanent housing.

Naomi found her first Nashville job while living there. She impressed newly successful syndicated television program producer Reg Churchwell immediately with both her good looks and her eagerness. She had been a detail person for the philanthropists and as an insurance agency secretary back in California, and she jumped right in to learn what she could about the video business. Churchwell helped her find a house to live in.

Far from the china doll of her youth, the dependent

woman of low self-esteem, Naomi had become strong. No weak sister could have thrown caution to the wind with two daughters in her charge and confidently floated around the country for weeks at a time just checking out the possibilities. Gypsy she may have been, but she was no drifter. Naomi had a purpose: to find her place in the sun, regardless of how insecure her life might seem to the folks back home.

"Mom has always been very adventurous," Wynonna said with pride. "There is such an incredible adventure streak in her that she has gone on for a long time."

Before the summer was out they had landed up in slow-moving, upscale, and historic Franklin. Their home was an old Victorian farmhouse with a barn and the narrow Harpeth River running through the backyard. It wasn't long before Naomi had set up a wringer washer on the back porch and begun making a new batch of lye soap. She and Wynonna wrapped the bars in pretty paper and used it as attention-getting gifts. That and the cherry red and white '57 Chevy became part of their trademark as Naomi began from the very first to calculate ways to become known around Nashville.

Franklin, Tennessee, is the most fashionable community among the many that surround Nashville on all sides. The town has a delightful core of attractive old commercial buildings, and at its residential core, a plethora of nineteenth-century homes. The central urban residential section of Franklin is somewhat similar to, though older than, the neighborhood where Naomi was raised among the lovely historic homes that surround Ashland's Central Park. But there are significant differences in the histories of those two cities. High up in the mountains of eastern Kentucky, hard by the Ohio River, Ashland had seen nothing like the fierce Civil War military action that raged across that prosperous little farming town south of Nashville more than 115 years before Naomi arrived.

The story of that fight is a fascinating background to the peculiar pride that today's residents' take in their history. Aptly named the battle of Franklin, it was the bloodiest battle of the Civil War in Tennessee. Confederate losses mounted to one of the worst casualty rates in what was probably the most unnecessarily bloody battle of that conflict.

On November 4, 1864, General John B. Hood, physically exhausted and apparently emotionally unhinged with frustration following a recent loss at nearby Spring Hill, ordered a poorly thought-out frontal attack against a heavily armed and well-entrenched Union force of perhaps twenty-five thousand men to his eighteen thousand bone-weary Confederate troops largely without artillery. Judicious historians call that battle order by Hood ill-advised; but it appears to have been the knee-jerk reaction of a nervous breakdown. In only five hours, Hood lost one third of his army to death, wounds, and capture. Robert E. Lee had fought the Seven Day campaign in Virginia earlier and in that week lost fewer men! Carter's Mill near Franklin ran red with the blood of rebel soldiers.

Today in Franklin you can still find bullet holes proudly preserved by their owners to commemorate that fight. Franklin citizens have not forgotten their moment in history, gory though it was. There are numerous painstakingly preserved historical sites in the town and an influential contingent of wealthy families with birth lines extending back to that time. Such is the town that served as the final incubator of the Judds' music.

The farming community surrounding Franklin is prosperous, though residential development has been eating away at the beauty of the countryside at a ravenous pace since the time Naomi arrived there. Naomi found one of the

landmark older houses, not yet tweaked by expensive historical renovation, and settled in.

Naomi hoped to make the most of her connection with
Churchwell's newly successful television production company. Churchwell is said to have taken a personal interest in
Naomi, who was full of brash desire to immediately make her
mark in the entertainment industry, but it quickly appeared
that he could do nothing for her. He reportedly took her to
Las Vegas to try to get her a break as an entertainer but found
no serious takers. She wasn't particularly talented at anything, and Wynonna was far too young.

Naomi left Churchwell's employ and went to file her
qualifications with the state nursing board. Nursing paid better and gave her more latitude in setting her schedule. She
could pull double shifts one week to earn overtime, then
spend time making contacts around the music business the
next. She began working shifts alternately between the old
Williamson County hospital and the one in nearby Murfreesboro, Tennessee. Confident in herself, Naomi did not despair.
There were plenty of new possibilities, including a semiregular slot on a local early morning television show hosted by
Ralph Emery.

Wynonna and Ashley attended new schools. Franklin
High School, where Wynonna started, was no ordinary farm
community educational institution. Williamson County remains the wealthiest of the counties surrounding Nashville
and Davidson County, and the student body and faculty reflected that reality. Some teachers and even more students
drove luxury cars to school. Teachers characterize the student body as mostly middle to upper-middle class in advantages and attitudes, with a healthy contingent of nouveaux
riches from Brentwood, the nearby bedroom community
built largely for Nashville's newer business and entertain-

ment successes. Franklin hosts the largest annual rodeo contest east of the Mississippi River, so naturally many youngsters owned their own horses and rode in competition.

At first tentatively seeking a niche in the student body, Wynonna joined the Pep Club and the Sportsman's Club. She played softball. She made a few good friends, but on the whole failed to establish herself within the cliques and clubs of the "school spirit" crowd. Materially comfortable as the students were, Wynonna had vastly broader life experience. She had little interest in western saddles and high-slung pickup trucks. Having been around so many creative, freethinking adults willing to treat her as an almost-adult, she had even less patience with the devouring insularity of the local teenage social scene. Her mind was already tracing the career her mother was grooming her for.

Few at Franklin High School (population sixteen hundred students) knew of her real name, and most of those only from younger sister Ashley, who dutifully went by Judd but told her guidance counselor that she was really a Ciminella. Wynonna Judd was a loner, but she managed to be well known just the same. Instead of the Casual Corner preppy fashions of the Brentwood set or the blue-jean look of the rodeo girls, Wynonna wore long skirts. She never wore cowboy boots. Having been exposed to so much adult strangeness in California, she was much more mature than most of her peers. It showed in the way she presented herself. Her tenth-grade English teacher referred to her hairdo as "very old for her age, matronly really."

"Wynonna always looked older; I think that had a lot to do with her makeup," explained school guidance counselor Bill Seifert. "Not that she wore too much, but she always made herself up to look more mature than the rest of the kids. You didn't see her in the halls acting silly or anything; she always acted like an adult."

Because she was different and because she now had her music to lose herself in, Wynonna made few friends. She had reached an age at which you either fit in or your peers ignore you. Most students at the school became aware that Wynonna was actually performing on "The Ralph Emery Show," but the wish to become a star, especially [in] country music, . . . was not one generally appreciated by the student body. "Every now and then one of the kids at school would come up and say . . . they'd seen me on TV," Wynonna recalled. "But even after that, it was still, 'Oh yeah, you're gonna be a star. You and a million others.' " She befriended a small group of girls who were a little on the wild side, who had their own headstrong styles that put them on the outside of the high-school mainstream. Kim McCarthy was one of that small group with whom Wynonna ran around.

"Wy was really like two people," Kim said. "In school she was real quiet, and she kept to herself a lot. She dressed different from all the kids at Franklin, like someone a lot older, and she wore a lot of makeup. That was one thing my mother didn't like about them was they wore a lot of makeup all the time. But she wanted to be different. She knew that a lot of kids talked about her behind her back, and even when they said things in front of her, it really hurt her feelings."

What some people at the school perceived as matronly fashion was in fact the forties and fifties look done on a budget. Naomi and Wynonna made fashion-shopping trips to the Salvation Army and Good Will stores to buy clothes, picking up the most interesting castoffs for their carefully concocted image. Instead of a new car, the sign of 'ultracool' at Franklin High, Wynonna drove her mother's red and white '57 Chevy to school some days.

There was a conscious striving at times to foster the appearance that mother and daughter might actually be sisters. Naomi always looked younger than her age; Wynonna often purposely dressed up to look older. Ralph Emery could rarely remember their odd names so early in the morning: he thought that they looked nearly the same age and he remembered Naomi telling tales of manufacturing homemade lye soap, so he called them the Soap *Sisters.*

"We did that show about once a month," Wynonna said. "It's funny because we would get up at 3:30 in the morning, be there by five, do it, and then I'd go to school. To get up at 3:30 and then go all day and not get out of school until 3 P.M. —you have to have a weird sense of humor for that."

"The first time we went on that show, I swear to God, we walked back in the dressing room and, of course, [nobody's] there," Naomi explained. "We hadn't even seen the show, we didn't know what all they did, and we weren't prepared. So we were standing in the dressing room down there in the basement of WSM; Dorothy [a program regular] came out of the restroom dressed up like a purple people eater. At five o'clock in the morning—hey, that's better than four cups of coffee to wake you up."

The girls' lack of musical training was a drawback when they tried to get the Emery show band to back their singing.

"I couldn't read music, and I didn't know how to write out a chart, so when we'd walk in, those musicians, I could just see those guys' faces," Wynonna confessed. "They would have their coffee and their newspapers, and it was like, oh, now we have to play this? We had to stand there and sing the song for them and go through it twice. But that was really the only experience we had as far as performing. I think it paid twenty-five dollars each time."

By eschewing the jeans and preppy fashions of most of her classmates, Wynonna was staking out her own uniqueness. Quiet, determined, focused more on her career aspirations and love of music, she managed to be unusual. With so much self-confidence, she later earned acceptance as a talented oddball, rather than cruel rejection. Wynonna, though every bit as dramatically oddball as her mother had been at an earlier age, was more open to hurt from the reactions of classmates than Naomi had been. Wynonna's peers hadn't known her all her life as had Naomi's classmates. They had no reason to accept without reservation her many idiosyncrasies.

Perhaps because of her oddness, perhaps because she didn't create time for the social scene, Wynonna didn't have a boyfriend in high school. Because she had lived in the West Coast film capitol and because she had an unquenchable thirst for her own eventual stardom, Wynonna earned the nickname Hollywood. The nickname that had so infuriated her mother in Morrill was proudly worn by the eldest daughter at Franklin High. When the name was used derisively, she learned to tune it out.

"She didn't let peer pressure bother her," said Mary Jane Wade, cheerleading squad sponsor, who taught the first-period psychology class to which Wynonna was often tardy. "It didn't bother her to go around with a guitar dressed like the fifties."

Wynonna was different, but she became almost proud of it. If there was confidence in that difference, there was also an absolute lack of shame in her lack of fashionable outfits or her mother's car. Wynonna knew it was a classic that had been used in *More American Graffiti*, even if it was only an old car to most of her classmates.

Naomi and Wynonna shopped the secondhand thrift stores for the forties and fifties skirts Wynonna loved because they couldn't afford to frequent trendy antique clothing stores. They could have dressed like everyone else—when Naomi worked regularly they weren't that poor—but they made a fashion statement out of their old clothes. It was one of many ways in which Wynonna stood out in the student body. Her sense of purpose alone set her apart. She knew by the time she was thirteen that she wanted to become a singing star. By fifteen she was actively pursuing it.

"She was outside-oriented," Seifert continued. "She didn't have time to be involved in school activities. . . . She was tardy to class about one or two days a week because she had been on 'The Ralph Emery Show.' "

Wynonna was sensitive about her television image in those early days. Her weight never really reached the obese stage, but her mother always seemed to make her feel fat anyway. That feeling hit her hard when an Emery show fan misidentified them in a way that seemed to point up her exaggerated sense of her size.

"Someone wrote in to Ralph Emery and asked about the Lard Sisters, and I wouldn't go to school that day," she said. "I stayed home and cried the whole day."

There was no way that she could slip in unnoticed on mornings when she arrived twenty minutes late after driving the nearly thirty miles back across Davidson County from the television studio. Having dropped Naomi off at the hospital staff entrance, she would pull into the Franklin High parking lot.

"A lot of kids from over in Brentwood who came here then drove the family Mercedes to school," said Tom Hankins, assistant principal of the school. "She drove that old '57 Chevy. That was the family car. I don't believe they had anything else."

After locking her guitar in the trunk, she would stop by the principal's office, where they no longer even put her on report for the infraction, then continue on her way to classes. Once there, she got by, but never really tried to excel. Sometimes, according to teachers, she took classes that required less work than she was capable of doing had she put her mind to it.

"She took a section of English that was considerably beneath her abilities, I think," said Wynonna's tenth-grade English instructor, Virginia Grimes. "She did that to give more time to her music. She did miss class a lot, but she always passed. . . . She was very serious, very mature and ladylike compared to most of the students her age. She never talked about aspirations in music a great deal, but you understood that it was her main interest."

Unwilling to approach Franklin High on its own terms, she relied on a small group of close friends. Still prone to candy bar binges after school, Wynonna was a wild child, but not a juvenile delinquent. Her mother was still too strict to allow her to get too out of hand. Given the atmosphere that Naomi was creating at her farmhouse—one of a winter camp for motel lounge bands—it is hard to imagine what else the girl could have become.

"When she got out of school her and me and another girl would go over to her house or go driving around Franklin in her mother's car, just cruising, and she was really wild," said Kim McCarthy. "I mean, we weren't really bad, but we gave our mothers fits. We really had some good times, but she was always thinking about music. When we'd go over to her house she'd get out her guitar and we'd be in her room and she'd start singing. Sometimes we'd stay overnight, and there was always somebody's bus in the back next to the barn and always musicians around."

As Wynonna's playing got better, so did her voice. At school Wynonna Judd was a quiet, big-boned girl who wore funky old clothes and did her hair up like a middle-aged woman; at home she was developing a powerful voice into a devastating instrument capable of blues inflections, experimenting with unique nuances.

She wasn't necessarily *being good*, however. Wynonna needed cash to go to the movies or just down to the local soda shop with one or two of her close friends. Since Naomi Judd was both a strict parent and a relatively uneven provider, Wynonna had to improvise for cash. Wynonna's mischievous side emerged in the pranks she pulled on her mother to get money for cruising adventures with her girlfriends. She figured a way to literally take the food out of her family's mouths to get her "hanging out" money.

"I used to take food back to Kroger [a grocery store], which is funny. I used to take food back . . . after we had shopped, to get money so I could go out on weekends. I only did it when I was desperate."

Naomi remembers that food often seemed to disappear from the shelves soon after she bought it. She can laugh at her daughter's antics now, but she wondered at the time where all the groceries were going. Had she known, she might have caused a scene. There were plenty of occasions when mother and daughter got into dramatic shouting and foot-stomping fights.

Ashley was coming into her own, but she was neither as close to her mother nor as likely to engage in hell-raising fights with her.

Ashley Ciminella agreed to use her mother's maiden name in school, though she did it mostly to keep down the confusion of having two names in the family. Known as Ashley Judd as she entered Franklin High as a freshman in 1983, she was no less striking in appearance than her older sister. In fact, she was, if anything, better looking. She has the thin figure and high cheekbones of her mother. Her talent, which Naomi encouraged, would be the same one that Naomi had rejected in Hollywood: modeling. In Franklin Ashley began modeling to earn money for her own clothes, and the styles she chose couldn't have been more different from those worn by Wynonna.

"Ashley would be one of the first ones in this part of the country to come in wearing the latest West Coast fashions," a teacher recalled. "Wynonna dressed plain, she was always twenty or thirty years behind, but Ashley was ahead of all the girls here. I think she got the clothes from modeling them."

It is interesting to hear Franklin High teachers compare the two Judd girls. Whereas Wynonna is remembered as serious, matronly, and not into dating but rather dedicated to a dream that few people were fully privy to, Ashley was outgoing, involved in school activities, fun-loving, and flirtatious with older boys.

"Ashley was real popular," guidance counselor Bill Seifert recalled. "She had time to be involved in school activities. Wynonna—if she wasn't in . . . class she was out trying to become a country-music star. See, most of the kids here liked hard rock at that time, and not too many were into the kind of music she was trying to do."

The younger Judd daughter wasted no time getting herself elected to the student council and the varsity cheerleading squad in her freshman year. She served on the makeup committee for a humorous play called *Frankenstein Slept Here.* Naomi was just as proud to support her achievements as she was to promote Wynonna's talent. Naomi wanted to see Ashley badly enough to use her most appealing smile to slip past the gate attendant at the homecoming football game, to photograph her youngest child as she shook her pom-poms with the other girls.

"I was at the gate and it cost $2.50 for tickets," Bill Seifert said. "Her mother came up and said, 'I just want to run in and take a picture of Ashley.' I never saw her again. Boy, I tell you, that burned me up. She still owes me that $2.50."

Naomi recalls that night for the effect her behavior had on Ashley.

"I remember that year at Homecoming when I took the camera and Ashley was cheerleading," she said, laughing. "She had a crush on this football player. I wanted to get some close-ups, but they were all down there on the field. I mean, this is my kid. I don't care if there are two thousand people out there watching, but she was down there on the field and the guy she had a crush on was standing there. I'm down there saying, 'Okay, can you do a pirouette now?' She just said, 'Mom!'"

Wynonna was not the only Judd to come in for Naomi's oft overbearing discipline. As proud as Naomi was of Ashley's accomplishment in getting elected cheerleader, she knew how much it meant to her daughter and used it to punish her for some adolescent infraction.

"Her mother came in [and] talked to me about it near the end of the [athletic] season," said Mary Jane Wade, the cheerleaders' sponsor that year. "Ashley had apparently told her mother a lie; she had caught her in a lie about something, and she grounded her from cheering the rest of the year. She came to me and said, 'I want her suspended from the cheerleaders for the rest of the year.' She missed the last six weeks of the basketball season because of it."

Ashley's withdrawal from the cheerleading squad was final. She'd have been able to return the next year, Naomi willing, but she would have had to attend cheerleader camp during the summer between her freshman and sophomore years. Instead, she chose a more international option and flew to Tokyo to spend the summer modeling clothing for Japanese clothes catalogs. Active in Nashville teen fashion modeling, she had been selected in competition by a scouting team from the Cosmo Agency in New York, which regularly combed the heartland for girls with that all-American look for chaperoned assignments to France, Tokyo, and other fashion hot spots. The experience, not to mention the money she earned, gave her a worldliness that no other girl at the country high school could match. Not even the Mercedes-driving children of Brentwood.

"The only thing I can say is that she was way ahead of everybody else," Mrs. Wade said about Ashley Judd. "Traveling to Japan was no big deal to her! She was very worldly.

"Most girls that age don't date that much, but Ashley had a very active social life, going out with boys who were mostly a couple of years older than her and mostly from other schools. She was fifteen and she had already done more things than most thirty-year-olds around here. She knew how to handle herself; she never met a stranger."

She was very much her mother's girl in those respects. The next year, Naomi kept her extracurricular activities to a minimum.

"Ashley [was] the only fifteen-year-old I know who subscribed to *Time* magazine and had her own money market account," Naomi explained. "Her teachers tell me that if she wants to be the first female president she could do it. She was cheerleader, she was Homecoming attendant, everything, but this year I kind of pulled the plug and said, 'You're going to do your chores and make straight A's and that's it.' "

Even after the experience as a professional juvenile fashion model in Japan, Ashley could mix right in with the other popular girls at Franklin High. Her worldliness was real; she had been there and back, so Franklin boys, whose greatest adventure might be riding in the junior rodeo, had little chance of really interesting her. She had reached the age where most girls have matured further socially than the boys in their class, but Ashley's poise and confidence made her more attractive.

It was different with Wynonna. Her confidence behind

her guitar grew at every appearance on "The Ralph Emery Show" and increased after an opportunity to sing before the music-business athletes of a popular charity golf tournament. But when it came to boys, Wynonna was a strikeout. She was usually dressed inappropriately for the classroom and too heavily made up to attract most boys at Franklin High. She experimented with her "look" too. One day she might wear a silk orchid behind her ear and affect the Maria Muldaur look; the next she might wear calf-length skirts, tease her hair and lacquer it into place, and look like one of the teachers—one of the frumpier ones at that. With ambitions in the country-music business—considered very tacky to the Franklin High student body—and an inexplicable penchant for funky frump, Wynonna was just "way out there."

E·I·G·H·T
Making Music City Listen

Naomi wasted little time in approaching the Nashville music industry in 1979. She was like a woman-child let loose in the promised land.

"What Mom did was put me in this environment—we lived in Franklin, which is thirty minutes from Nashville—so she could keep her pulse on the music industry—" Wynonna began to tell one reporter.

"Finger on the pulse," Naomi corrected her with a raised eyebrow.

"—finger on the pulse of the industry while I was in high school," Wynonna continued. "She'd go down to Music Row and meet people, and she was aware of what was going on."

Her Hollywood days had taught her the value as well as the drawbacks of being an attractive single woman, and Polly had always taught her to put her best foot forward. Combining those lessons, Naomi dolled herself up to the nines when she went out to call on people she hoped could help her. She typically overdressed, and only the visage of Tammy Faye

Bakker would supplant the memory of her makeup style; but she did it innocently: still a small-town girl playing dress-up.

Dramatics had been her style since grammar school, and she was learning to use her assets to get what she wanted. What she wanted was attention. Sure, shallow California playboys had been drawn to her good looks and aura of vulnerability as to a magnet. She learned quickly how to tell what made a man interested in her. She also learned how to play off their interests, to open doors in the business for herself, usually dancing just out of reach. Few men could remain unaffected by her figure and her stunning mane of brunet hair. She often dressed to emphasize her attributes, and why not? She had learned how to use her good looks to disarm men. It became as much a tool of self-defense as a calling card: the mother in her midthirties who looked better, sometimes almost younger, than her teenage daughter.

She also carried away from Hollywood the memory of that film script left in her windshield wipers by an ardent admirer. She was bubbling over with energy and naïveté, but her brash ambition struck many people as predatory. They would see a woman who wouldn't take no for an answer. Dressed to kill and flashing that big smile, Naomi's limited free time could be used efficiently on Music Row, which is concentrated in a four block area of Sixteenth, Seventeenth, Eighteenth, and Nineteenth Avenues South in Nashville. For the would-be songwriter, singer, or musician, Music Row is as convenient as a shopping mall of entertainment enterprises. Naomi could hit a half dozen offices in an afternoon. Her ideas in the first year or so in Nashville still ran to making something of herself, at least until Wynonna was ready. Wynonna, after all, wasn't even old enough to drive legally when they first hit town. She felt that she was now close to realizing the dream of center stage that she had harbored since childhood, but she was still unschooled in the realities of the entertainment business. It didn't take long for her to start getting an education.

"I was taking my day off from the hospital, and my girlfriends who worked in record companies used to give me promo LPs to play," Naomi recalled. "I'd hear producers [styles] and try to find out what was going on."

"I think she could walk into someone's office and know whether they were interested in her as a woman or as a professional musician," said Wynonna.

It was by now a practiced skill, indeed.

"It's amazing how many doors I actually got through," Naomi recalled. "You know what I think did it, what caught the jaded attention of those people? I'd walk in with our tape and I'd be all dressed up in my Sunday dress, all bright-eyed, and say 'My daughter and I sing together.' And they'd say, 'What do *you* do?' And I'd say, 'Well this is my day off. I'm a registered nurse in a county hospital.' I ran into a lot of producers, a lot of label guys who'd say, 'Let's go talk about it over dinner.' And I'd say, 'No, I have to go home and fix dinner for my kids.' I wanted them to listen to our music. I let it be known that I had enough confidence in what we wanted to do that we'd only do it on our terms.

"There were two producers, who I won't name, but I'd walk into their office, they'd sit back in their chairs with their cigars and say, 'Well, I'm booked today, but how 'bout coming away with me for the weekend and we'll discuss your music, honey,'" Naomi continued. "Some day I'll write a book and burn them all in hell!"

This made Naomi mad, but she didn't let things like that drag her down. She was hardly a prude, but she insisted on controlling this as well as every other aspect of her life. Neither did she limit her ambitions strictly to being Wynonna's singing partner, sensing a world of opportunities in Nashville's entertainment industry. Sparkling with naive enthusiasm, Naomi concocted a number of half-thought-out plans to break into the business, including one about which she approached Robert K. Oermann (now music reporter for the Nashville *Tennessean* and *USA Today)* and John Lomax III, then both working at the Country Music Foundation Library.

"In 1979, when I was working down at the CMF, Naomi came down and tried to get us to write a script for a radio-program idea she had that revolved around the history of country music," Lomax said. Lomax was a good man to approach on the subject. He was named for his grandfather, John A. Lomax, who was a famous country, blues, and folk music scholar, associated notably with the establishment of the Library of Congress folklore collection. John A. Lomax discovered famed blues performer Huddie "Leadbelly" Ledbetter in a Mississippi prison and got him released to record. He and his son Alan Lomax recorded Leadbelly and wound up co-writing or publishing the main body of that famed songwriter's musical output, including the classic country-blues number "Goodnight Irene" and "Midnight Special."

"We used to get people coming in wanting us to do stuff like that for them for no money all the time, and you just had to tell them no," Oermann said.

"Basically, she had this idea, but she didn't have any backers or any idea really of what to do with it," Lomax continued. "She wanted us to write it on spec [recording industry jargon for 'in the speculation of someday being paid']. She was real cheerful and intelligent, but she had no idea what she was up against in trying to get it produced, syndicated, and marketed."

The impression she gave was that of an operator, a woman with a lot of guts and gumption who was being a fill-in nurse to lend a little stability to her uncertain life as she tried to make it big. One of the first things she did when she began to grasp some of the elements of success in that industry was to draft her own one-page biography. She had been so taken by the story and performances in *Coal Miner's Daughter,* the film based on Loretta Lynn's autobiography, that she gave her own life a similar spin, emphasizing Kentucky and her "genteel poverty" and rural experiences for more Butcher's Holler ambiance than it deserved—all to create an aura of Appalachian glamour, complete with references to her lye soap. She more or less made them sound like the Beverly Hillbillies, but then every trip to California had impressed her more with the rock-solid importance of her Kentucky background. Californians were enthralled with the trappings of her childhood's rural relatives. She knew it was a hot image.

"Before I went to Hollywood, I thought everybody knew how to raise a garden and about country living," she said. "I started appreciating how lucky we were to be from Kentucky, to know how to take care of ourselves and have priorities in life. If we hadn't left Ashland to go to Hollywood, we would never have appreciated our Appalachian heritage so much."

Naive and ambitious, having a bio to hand out gave her confidence that she was making a professional presentation. It was a short sketch that was more public-relations sheet than résumé, but as she refined it through the next few years, it helped her focus on those image elements she thought gave her and Wynonna more appeal. It represented them as she idealized them, as her dramatic sense of reality helped her condense her thirty-plus years of dreaming and wandering. She walked it into studios and publishing offices to give substance to her ambitions.

"All I remember is she showed up at the Sound Shop one day," said Jon Shulenberger, who gave her the first serious shot at the business in Nashville. He didn't realize until later that Naomi had first walked in off the street and represented herself as a singer to his partner in Sound Shop Productions, a commercial jingle production house. Claiming to have performed at California's Palomino Club—though she had no demo tapes to back up her claim—she boldly asked to be considered as a jingle singer. Perhaps she had reconsidered that braggadocio, or more likely she had forgotten she had even popped in there before—she stuck her head in anywhere people would let her past the receptionist's desk.

"She had just come from California when I started working with her," as Shulenberger explained the glossed-over image that was part of Naomi's energetic promotion of herself and Wynonna. "The story was vague but she worked for someone who was very wealthy out in San Francisco or something. She presented me with a résumé, but the more I looked at it, it was not a résumé at all. She was creating an image of herself in a PR way even then. She painted a picture of herself and her daughter, and whether it was all factual or not, it was basically a good PR job. It was projecting an image, and a colorful one, to the extent that their roots went back to the Kentucky Mountains. It was in a perspective that she thought was merchandisable. It took a while for me to realize that the author of it was Naomi."

She talked Shulenberger into giving them a listen, for the first time really representing herself and Wynonna as a mother and daughter duet team. As part of the package, he agreed to listen to some tunes Naomi had written. By the time she met Shulenberger, she had made other, at least glancing contacts in the music business. She dropped names to impress him. She mentioned in conversation that she had made friends with Chet Atkins, former head of RCA in Nashville and still one of the most influential men at that label at that time. That was a promising sign, he thought, though not every would-be starlet who caught Chet's attention wound up with a recording contract at RCA.

Shulenberger was looking for someone to produce as a recording artist just then. He wanted to expand from his base as a jingle producer; the Judds might just fit the bill. When they both arrived to meet with him the first time, he was impressed by their style: dressed in forties clothing and driving that snazzy '57 Chevrolet with the new novelty license tag that read REDHOT 2. No subtlety there, just eye-catching style.

"The girls came in their red and white '57 Chevy and they created an aura about them," Shulenberger recalled. "Naomi didn't drive around town in a car that you could lose in a crowd. They were a pretty interesting pair, and I decided there was probably something there to work with."

A one-year development contract was drawn up. Naomi thought that signing a contract meant that she was halfway there, but it wasn't that easy. Shulenberger was, at that time, part owner of the Sound Shop Studios, so it was no trouble to book a session to give them a tryout. Still, it takes time for a new act to actually get to the stage of recording in master sessions, the level at which release-quality work is done. First they had to try out Wynonna's voice on a variety of songs to see what suited her best. Since she was only fifteen and sixteen during the year that she worked with Shulenberger, the idea was to try her in either the "little girl" vein or as a teenage vamp à la Tanya Tucker. In the music business they call such a scattershot approach "throwing it up against the wall to see if anything sticks."

Before doing any master sessions that they could offer to major record labels, Shulenberger set up an "open mike" session that would give Naomi and Wynonna a chance to show him and production partner Mike Bradley what their sound should be, at the same time previewing Naomi's work as a songwriter. In doing so, Shulenberger created what may someday be released as a treasure of early-Judds recordings.

These recordings are a series of simple guitar and vocals done as they normally sang: primarily two voices accompanied by Wynonna's guitar. Captured on tape were a couple of standard country and gospel tunes the Judds had in their performance repertoire and some Naomi originals that have never been recorded anywhere else. The sound of their voices blending in 1980 was crisp, unusual, and completely astounding. Had Shulenberger's ears been open for a new direction in music rather than the formula that country radio was then accepting, he might have discovered the simple acoustic western- and mountain-tinged harmonies that are the center of the Judds' sound today.

But someone else, someone Naomi knew as it turned out, would have to break ground for the eighties crop of "new traditionalists." It was really Ricky Skaggs's Top 20 breakthrough with his rocking electric version of the old Lester Flatt number "Don't Get Above Your Raisin' " in 1981 that began slowly to open the doors to traditional country sounds such as the Judds, George Strait, Randy Travis, and Reba McEntire, among others, that have dominated the mideighties country charts. When Shulenberger was recording Wynonna as a solo artist, country radio was awash in a polluted river of pop-crossover mishmash characteristic of the so-called urban cowboy era. Naomi and Wynonna already had their sound down, though their delivery was far from polished.

Naomi's own tunes were melodically sophisticated, though the lyrics lacked professional finesse. Most surprising on that tape is the degree to which the Judds' image through song topics had already taken shape. "Lazy Country Evening," by Naomi, was a duet with a western, Sons of the Pioneers type of harmony, based on the theme of a happy rural family. Wynonna talked Bradley into going back and letting her add a third high harmony part that really filled out the vocal track, forerunning a studio technique that they still utilize today. "My Mama Says" tells a story from Wynonna's mouth that old-fashioned girls have more fun. "Daddy Are You Comin' Home Tonight" has a traditional mountain-country sound dealing with the dangers of working in the coal mines around Hazard, Kentucky. From these it is apparent that the family values of Mama and Kentucky that would emerge in such Judd hits as "Mama He's Crazy" and "Why Not Me" were already being worked out in Naomi's mind as important themes in their music.

The last duet was a traditional country hymn entitled "Softly and Tenderly, Jesus Is Calling." Their harmonies were loose but impressive as they passed the melody from Naomi's low register to Wynonna's high line as it pleased them. Listening to this work, it is plain in retrospect that the duet would have been the most advantageous use of either woman's voice. But no one at Sound Shop saw any likelihood of selling them that way. To finish the session, Wynonna soloed on a tune called "(But until Then) I've Got Time on My Hands" and on a tune from Linda Ronstadt's repertoire, "Silver Blue." The latter seemed to Shulenberger to indicate the direction he should take.

"It showcased Wynonna more than any other they did that day," he explained. "It just had that special quality that said this girl is going to make it. It was more Wynonna that we thought we were working with. At her age she was really where Brenda Lee had been, and I thought that she had potential to really do something. She showed a lot of talent at a really early age."

Much to Naomi's chagrin, their first break seemed to exclude her. She sat quietly in the studio and watched Shulenberger work with Wynonna, but she continued to promote them around town as a duo.

"She wanted the sessions built around her and her songs

as a duet, but we dismissed Naomi as part of the project,"
Shulenberger explained. "In retrospect you can see she knew
what she was talking about."

Naomi saw Shulenberger's efforts as an opportunity, as a
step in the right direction, even if it varied from her vision of
the act. She patiently continued her other efforts on their
behalf, keeping in close touch with Chet Atkins. She also
drew on Ricky Skaggs for encouragement and introductions
around town, as he had by that time quit Emmylou Harris's
band and was in the middle of making his own deal with Epic
Records.

"I always felt the mom was the salesman," Shulenberger
observed about Naomi's hustle. "She had more drive and
determination than anyone I had ever met in the business. It
was clear to me . . . on that basis alone that they would
make it to some degree in the music business."

Meanwhile, Wynonna was struggling through high
school. Petite Ashley continued modeling to buy the latest
fashions before they reached the local stores, in contrast to
Wynonna's heavyset, thrift-store Andrews Sister look. Their
mother compared the two in terms of worldliness and cleanliness, but what emerges is a contrast in emotional makeup.

"Ashley's sophisticated; she goes to art galleries and
keeps her room clean," Naomi observed. "She's just the op-
posite of Wynonna. You need a tetanus shot to get into Wynonna's room!"

High school was Ashley's medium. Though modeling
and her international travel gave her vastly superior self-
confidence, she didn't lord it over her peers. She fit in because it was important to her. Wynonna, on the other hand,
wanted only music badly enough to pursue it. Her main
social outlets among her peers were her few girl friends, with
whom she cruised Franklin, went roller skating, and had
pajama parties. Otherwise, she was surrounded by adults

from "The Ralph Emery Show" band, Shulenberger and his associates, and the members of the band Memphis. Memphis made their off-the-road home at the Judds' when Naomi began a long-term on-again-off-again relationship with one of their members, Larry Strickland.

To say the least, Wynonna was different from most young people her age. Even her best friends didn't understand the wide spectrum of music that she had been exposed to and how it all combined to become a part of her.

"My dad taught me Bonnie Raitt and the blues, my mom taught me bluegrass and old mountain harmonies, and my grandparents taught me big band and swing," she recalled. "So, I was fifteen and sixteen and my friends were listening to hard rock, and everybody would invite me to a party and say, 'Don't bring your records.' "

Wynonna worked hard on her music that year, as the Sound Shop sessions loomed and the business of shopping the master tapes they were going to do approached. Naomi created a relaxed atmosphere at home that emphasized their love for music, surrounding herself with musicians and young songwriters that she'd met in her Music Row forays. Shulenberger sometimes came out to dinner, bringing his own daughter to play with Ashley while he, Naomi, Wynonna, and whoever else might drop in passed the guitar around the kitchen table for hours on end. Sometimes they would engage in highly animated discussions of what they planned to do next to break into the big time. When Naomi's scheming got on a roll, Shulenberger's attention sometimes drifted off toward his daughter and Ashley at play. He noted that even if she couldn't sing, the younger Judd child had a creative streak of her own.

"They would make up their own soap operas on audio tape while the Judds worked on career development in the other room," he recalled. "They were really quite cute; they made up their own commercials and everything. I was kind of surprised that Ashley took such a backseat role in that family as she did."

Through all the career planning sessions, Wynonna became impatient. She thought that she was ready to "come out" as a professional long before Naomi would let her. She knew kids who formed bands and played around Nashville in rock 'n' roll nightclubs like Cantrell's and The Cannery. They were minor local celebrities. When Naomi took her to a showcase performance for the band Memphis, it was all she could do to keep Wynonna off the stage so that her boyfriend's band could show their stuff to prospective record labels. By the end of her junior year Wynonna was ready to explode, but Naomi continued to hold her back for the big time. With Wynonna's emotional personality, Naomi had to watch from week to week to see how seriously her daughter would take her career potential. She didn't want the girl to waste it all for a couple of dollars in some smoky rock 'n' roll dive. The rock 'n' roll scene was synonymous with casual sex and drug abuse to Naomi, not to mention poor hygiene.

"Well, Wynonna wanted to sing and get into a band even when she was still in high school, but I didn't want to let her," Naomi told Patrick Carr for *Country Music* magazine. "I didn't want her to be just another one of those scrungy club kids, you know?

"But she pushed and pushed, and I did a deal with her. I told her that once she graduated high school, I'd go into it with her. That way I could be sure she didn't get involved with the wrong sort of people, go nowhere, and end up teasing hair in a beauty parlor the rest of her life. I know what that's all about. You can blow your whole life at an age when you're just thinking about your next milk shake."

Naomi continued to make the rounds of Music Row, traveling in their attention-getting automobile, always trying to make an impression, always succeeding. Sometimes she and Wynonna would make the scene together.

"When she came in I think she wore Jungle Gardenia perfume, if you've ever smelled that," Shulenberger recollected. "The girls upstairs could tell that Naomi was here and would inform me without even looking downstairs."

The impression she made disarmed men, but it also put a lot of women off. Wives saw her as their worst nightmare: the predator, the dolled-up other woman. If they had to compete for their husband's attentions with Naomi, they would never have a spare moment the rest of their lives.

"My wife came in [one] Christmas, and Wynonna and Naomi walked in the door," Shulenberger recalled with a chuckle, though he admits it wasn't so funny at the time. "As always they liked to wear Andrews Sisters forties-style clothing, and you never saw Naomi with a hair out of place, with her guard down. She always wore a lot of makeup. My wife was in sweat pants, took one look, and walked back outside again. Everyone felt underdressed when Naomi came in."

Shulenberger and Bradley finally discarded Naomi's tunes in their search for material to have Wynonna record. They had tried to record one, but it was just too quirky for a bunch of free-lance session musicians to decipher in a three-hour session.

"We tried to cut one of the songs in the studio, but it just didn't fall into place," Shulenberger explained. "It was more like the stuff they are doing now with the slightly western tone to the harmonies. But they were a little odd for the studio musicians to pick up on."

Naomi bowed to their decision as a matter of practicality, but only as far as Shulenberger's sessions were concerned. Otherwise, she seemed to work almost at cross-purposes with his plan. She determined to keep control of the rest of her daughter's career direction and never really abandoned her original ideas for the two of them.

"She would let Wynonna have the spotlight in our sessions if it meant getting to the labels and into the studio," said Shulenberger. "I think she kept her dreams in the back of her mind and never forgot where she wanted to wind up."

He called on Music Row publishers for material for Wynonna to record. It is lesson 1 in the *Famous Songpluggers Guide to Keeping Your Job* that an unknown artist with neither a record-label deal nor a big-name producer doesn't have access to the best new compositions of last year's CMA songwriter of the year. Still, Shulenberger managed to round up four songs that he thought were worth taking into the studio. One was by Red Lane and two had been written by Deborah Allen, who later came to the fore as a Capitol and RCA Records act herself. Nervous about the session, Wynonna looked tired when she and her mother showed up. She had been binging on candy bars again and her face was broken out.

Shulenberger hired some of the best pickers and backup singers for the session. Rather than let Naomi sing with Wynonna, he brought in Lea Jane Berinati, Mike Black, Jozef Nuyens and his sister Mimi Nuyens. The Nuyens family had recently bought a Franklin studio and relocated from their Netherlands home, where they had been the European equivalent of the Osmonds or the Singing King Family. Berinati was a contractor who regularly supplied backup groups called the Lea Jane Singers, out of which Janie Fricke would emerge as a solo artist. They cut no corners on the musicians either. Players included well-known session musicians Shane Keister (keyboards), Brent Rowan (guitar), and Sonny Garrish (steel guitar).

The first of the four songs he had Wynonna record was "Some of Us," written by Red Lane. For fans of arcane musical facts, it can be noted that this is the only instance in Wynonna Judd's body of recorded work that includes an extended narration. She talks and sings her way through this sentimental number about a teenage girl coming in at 3 A.M. and confounding her parents by thanking them for their concern and for trusting her.

"No Aces" (writer unknown) was a clichéd country ditty using a deck of cards as a metaphor for life in a three-way love affair in which Wynonna was the loser. Definitely an adult treatment, it is the only "cheatin'" song that Naomi ever let her daughter attempt. She preferred the profamily themes. Touching on the little girl element of Wynonna's actual age, "I'm Afraid of the Dark," by Deborah Allen, was a hauntingly minor-key melody, with Wynonna pulling back on her vocal strength to produce an almost childish tone in a straightforward puppy-love heartache number.

"We were trying to position her with this one as a little girl," said Shulenberger. "The others were more mature themes, and she used a woman's voice to sing them."

Of the tunes that they cut that afternoon, Deborah Allen's "Wishing Won't Make It So" became the one that Shulenberger pushed in trying to get a deal. It was a pop-flavored rocker, sort of a Bonnie Raitt meets Electric Light Orchestra treatment that pulled a strong edge from Wynonna's voice similar to her later performance on the hit "Have Mercy." None of the master sessions or the open-mike numbers compare in polish or strength to the Judds' commercial releases, but none of it is actually bad. When the Judds' career output is firmly established, these recordings will be collectors items offering fascinating insights into the early development of their sound. They were not deemed so valuable when they were fresh, however.

"Basically we shopped the material around town—saw just about everybody in town—and there was a hesitancy to take on a young girl," Shulenberger explained. "There were a lot of problems that I hadn't realized from a record company's point of view in development of an underaged girl."

He got one refusal after another. He even got turned down by Jimmy Bowen, who was then heading Elektra Records' country office in Nashville, despite the fact that he presented Wynonna and Naomi together for a live audition as a duet after the tapes got an ambivalent response. He found that he simply could not control Naomi once they got into an interview with a label executive; nor could he keep her from coming along.

"They went into Bowen's office," Shulenberger said, chuckling. "Wy took her guitar and sang, Mom did backups, and Jimmy just didn't hear it. They all had their chance, and some of them, like Jimmy, had a real good shot at it because they were essentially doing the same thing they wound up doing now."

RCA, then headed by Jerry Bradley, heard Wynonna and passed, as did Dimension Records, whose owner would later become the Judds' manager. Though Shulenberger got turned down at the record companies when he pitched Wynonna as an artist, he got plenty of follow-up calls from various people wanting Naomi's home phone number.

"Nobody was after Wynonna—she was jail bait—but Naomi had that aura of vulnerability sometimes," he explained. "As far as the artist thing, nobody wanted to take the responsibility of an underaged girl, or they wanted to be involved for the wrong reasons."

Naomi's intrusive involvement in record label meetings threw Shulenberger a curve. She often stole the show from Wynonna, and intentionally or not, her ability to disarm often obstructed serious negotiations. If there was ever any chance of selling Wynonna as a solo singer, Naomi decreased it.

"Anytime we'd go in somewhere the limelight would

always be on Naomi, which constantly undercut my trying to pitch Wynonna as an artist," Shulenberger sighed. "It's difficult when you walk in a door with an artist and her mother radiates all the charisma and charm. I was trying to sell Wynonna to these executives, but Naomi was right there and they couldn't figure out what to focus on."

Time was running out on the year, and Shulenberger and Bradley brainstormed in one more wrong direction.

"We didn't think Judd—well, it was country and authentic, but it wasn't a very glamorous name," he said.

It was a valid criticism at the time: the next outfit to try to sell the act ran into similar problems on a public-relations level.

"We wanted to sell Wynonna on using her first name. Sylvia was the only one doing that at that time, but she was not then and is not now a household name. We thought that Wynonna was better than Wynonna Judd. The mistake that we made was—well, let's just say we made a mistake.

"We had a year's contract, and when I was unable to sell product at the end of the year, I didn't want to hold the girls back. I think what set us back there was that the thing that was most salable in the group was the uniqueness of the mother and daughter, but the daughter was too young and nobody wanted the mother—as an artist."

Shulenberger was glad to get rid of them, in a way. Naomi had somehow pulled him into duties that far outstripped the job of record producer, and it was wearing him out.

"It was more work than it should have been," he recounted of that year when he had them under contract. "Keeping up with Naomi was a problem. She was always looking for an angle, always looking to book them here and there, and I always seemed to be going along as an agent. I'm not sure she asked me to do that, but I wound up doing it to see what they were up to and what she was doing."

What Naomi was doing was making sure that she and Wynonna got on every important stage they could. Her boyfriend talked his band into letting them open a showcase performance they had arranged for a lot of important radio personalities during October's Country Music Week one year. Naomi talked her way (with Chet Atkins' help) into a slot entertaining celebrities at the Roy Acuff Pro/Celebrity Golf Tournament.

"My time involved with the Judds was more as talent agent than producer . . . ," Shulenberger explained. "It was a role I was uncomfortable with. They dragged me out to the Roy Acuff golf tournament to perform. Naomi had worked the deals to perform at these types of programs. We got out to the Roy Acuff golf tournament at Henry Horton State Park and sat through this thing with Chet Atkins.

"It came time for them to perform, and somehow they had been left off the list. There was a moment of panic because this is why they were there. The emcee was a Nashville deejay I knew named Dick Kent, and he slid them into the program. There was a big round of applause because they were so unique. For the rest of the show we sat with Chet Atkins, and as we left, it was with Roy Acuff and his wife."

Naomi made more points with Acuff when his wife was accidentally hit by a collapsing bookcase on the way out. Naomi cleared everyone away, protesting that she was a nurse and would take care of the woman, which she did while a variety of celebrities looked on.

"At a certain point in late '79 or '80 I realized [working with the Judds] was taking up too much of my time and pushing me into roles I had no expertise in," said Shulenberger, who released the Judds from their contract. "I called Patsy Bruce, who was representing her husband Ed Bruce and Nat Stuckey, but she didn't have any females on her roster. She took them on for a while. I think she tried to use Naomi for some jingle voice-overs."

Naomi Judd's voice didn't stand on its own, especially for voice-overs. But Patsy Bruce had other business sidelines besides keeping her cowboy husband, Ed Bruce, out of trouble and in the charts. Among her many talents are business convention planning and film casting. Her casting credentials began to build after she successfully placed her husband in a television mini-series and then in a regular feature role in James Garner's short-lived update of the "Maverick" series. She was also connected with the people who cast the film *Urban Cowboy.*

The same egoless capacity for hard work that had made Naomi valuable to the Lucas film crew as a production secretary recommended her to Patsy Bruce. Patsy put Naomi to work as a hostess in a number of her costume-themed convention parties and kept it in the back of her mind that the woman had been a speaking extra in *More American Graffiti.*

"I used Naomi for so much over a period of two or three years because I always found her more than willing to work to keep herself in show business and the kids eating," Patsy Bruce observed. "I put her in a big old antebellum hoop skirt for one insurance company conference, and all the top executives wanted their pictures made with her. Nothing I did made Naomi Judd a star, but I wish I could find people who were that willing to work. If I didn't admire her for anything else, I would admire her for that. I think that is the reason she is a star."

With the Sound Shop sessions behind them, Naomi had at least been personally exposed to every important record company in Nashville, and a few that weren't. Had she done nothing else except stir up contacts and opportunities in the next three years, she would have had a full-time job. But she had two full-time jobs already: nursing and mothering.

Raising the same rebellious teenager whose career she was trying to promote made things twice as hard on the mother-daughter relationship, adding to Naomi's burdens. She had always been a strict parent; now she was becoming a hard-driving career director as well. There were times when Wynonna bucked ferociously at the dual control her mother was exercising over her, which only made Naomi assert her authority more. That's just the kind of people they both were.

Naomi loved being in and around the music business, and so she made her boyfriend and his band practically extended live-in family when they were in town. When they were on the road for weeks at a time, she often drove into Nashville after an evening shift at the old Williamson County Hospital for a drink at one of the Music Row area bars, where she might run into someone she knew. Coming straight from work after stopping briefly to check in on the girls, she is remembered by many people as coming in after midnight, dressed in her hospital uniform, her hair as perfect as a beauty parlor ad. In a dimly lit bar like the old Close Quarters Hotel, which filled up with pickers and music business personnel—whose days didn't get started until midafternoon anyway—that lone beauty all in white was hard to miss. That's another of the strong images Naomi Judd left in the minds of many in the music business.

N·I·N·E

The Breakthrough

Nineteen eighty-one would be a year of hard work and vague hopes, after the Judds' affiliation with Jon Shulenberger ended with no record deal. If the truth were known, Naomi hadn't counted on that deal. Insinuating herself into every presentation that Shulenberger tried to make of Wynonna as a solo act was Naomi's way of trying to turn that into an opportunity for them both: not Wynonna but the *Judds*. She hung her real hopes on the exposure she was generating for them as a duo. They continued to appear on "The Ralph Emery Show," though it was little more than a grandly staffed farm report. She continued to ply strangers with tapes of the two of them, often to the general embarrassment of everyone.

"I went to a showcase for her boyfriend's band, Memphis," said Nashville independent record promoter Stan Byrd, who was then head promoter for Warner Bros. Records country division. "She was standing practically accosting people as they were on the way out: 'I've got this tape; you wanna listen to my tape?' I just ducked my head and slid out. There's just so much of that, you learn to block it out."

It wasn't the best Music Row etiquette, but etiquette doesn't break through the wall of cynicism that record industry veterans build up for self-protection over years of frontal assaults by talentless want-to-be's who haunt the office lobbies and watering holes of the business. Naomi's relentless ambition was built on her faith in the uniqueness of the Judd sound. She often dragged an enthusiastic but completely overshadowed Wynonna along with her. Ashley was typically brought along as well, though seemingly only for lack of a sitter.

"Ashley was always the one in the other room while Wynonna and I sat and practiced on our guitar at home," Naomi confessed. "She was the one who would sit in the front office at WSM while we did 'The Ralph Emery Show' and wait in the car while we would go and audition for somebody."

Naomi hustled contacts where she could get them, making friends where she could and getting as many people as possible to listen. It was often easier to make friends.

"She knew exactly what she wanted," Patsy Bruce observed. "There's only two ways to make that happen. It has to be the one most important thing in your life, and you have to have a mentor to hold your hand and open the doors. I've never known a superstar that didn't have that focus. You have to be willing to do anything that it takes; anything. And she had that kind of focus. People who say there's something wrong with that are wrong; that's just what it takes. Just like people will do anything it takes to become a doctor or a lawyer."

It would appear that Chet Atkins filled some of the role of early Nashville mentor for Naomi. But the old guard was on the wane at his primary power base: RCA. Joe Galante was the rising star executive at the label. Atkins's biggest break as a record producer had come from Steve Sholes in the late fifties: he became active manager of the office when Sholes was promoted to New York, and got the title of Nashville division vice president in 1968. Atkins had given up the administrative headaches of label chief to Jerry Bradley, son of Owen Bradley, who had built the first recording studio on Music Row in the early fifties and headed Decca Records' country division. Bradley was thus heir to a mighty country-music family and sympathetic to Atkins and the old guard. When Jerry Bradley stepped down from RCA in 1982, Galante was elevated to replace him. It was a moment when Music Row changed its style and tempo forever.

Joe Galante was the ultimate replacement for the Nashville ruling families. He was young and aggressive, and he was not one of them. Galante was no good ole boy. He was a New Yorker who worked his way up from the accounting department. His primary vision was one of numbers, of the bottom line. He was not a record man or a musician like the Bradleys and Atkins, nor did he owe allegiance to a thirty-year-old system of help-your-buddy that kept such established power figures and their families and friends in the record business. Galante was a number cruncher who favored a more highly pressured, efficient staff and system of operating than had been the Nashville norm. Working at a record label in the Galante era might never be as much fun as it had been before. The Music City pioneers took that attitude with them as they moved out of control of the major labels, setting up their own offices and studios as headquarters for their still considerable influence and involvement.

As Galante's star rose over RCA, Atkins's own dimmed as a force there. Galante was young and ambitious and, in his midthirties, the youngest man to head a major label in Nashville. He wanted complete control over the label, and Atkins, who still recorded for RCA, must have challenged that status with his old connections and the general industry view that RCA Nashville was the label that Chet had built. Atkins was quietly in Naomi's corner, but even he could see that the act wasn't ready in 1981. RCA artist-development executive Jerry Flowers was vocal in his championship of the duo to label brass, but he was another remnant of the Bradley era that Galante was relentlessly rooting out. Politics worked against the Judds for the time being, and Wynonna was still underage, regardless of where they went. Naomi's ambitions were stifled for the time being—for at least another year, when Wynonna would turn eighteen.

Although she had learned to make herself look and act like an adult—sometimes more so than her mother—Wynonna still felt the sting of rejection at Franklin High. Just as she was deeply hungry for professional acceptance in the music industry, she wanted recognition from her classmates that she was more than just "that weirdo Wynonna who dresses funny." She wanted their applause. For Wynonna, after those early attempts at fitting in, high school offered only one forum to establish herself: the annual student talent contest.

Wynonna was the most self-assured of the contestants on the Franklin High School auditorium stage competing in the spring 1981 student talent show. Behind her guitar, she was in her own element. Knowing that the rock 'n' roll tastes of the students ran from heavy metal to the Charlie Daniels' Band, she pulled from the Eagles (the preeminent country-rock group of the seventies) "Desperado" and won the blue ribbon. But the win was no fairy-tale conversion of the unbelievers. According to several teachers, Wynonna was heckled. Heavy-metal fans, with their spiky hairdos—never the type to push the ballad button on the jukebox—thought

"Desperado" was sentimental mush. According to teachers, a handful of black students, unhappy at being bused into the unfamiliar culture of the mainly rural all-white high school in the first place, added their disapproving catcalls to the hubbub.

It was Wynonna's first challenge as a developing concert performer, and she passed the test. Her ability to smile and wave confidently as the prize was awarded to her brought the applause she had wanted so badly, applause that finally drowned out the hecklers. She was caught in limbo on Music Row, but Wynonna had earned the respect, if not the admiration, of a majority of her classmates. She was featured in a section of the yearbook dedicated to recognizing "special people." She earned the title "most talented" in class voting, and her first-place award in the contest was duly recorded. Most interesting, though, was the line Wynonna herself added to the citation stating her ambitions in life. She stated that her goals were "to live each day to its fullest. To be constructive and creative and to be successful in the music business (in other words, rich and famous!)."

That talent show in the spring of 1981 was the last Wynonna Judd would be able to enter as an amateur.

"Her last year, she was in [the talent show]; but by that time she was a pro, and everyone agreed that she could be in it, but she couldn't compete," said high-school counselor Bill Seifert. "She wore stage costumes to school a lot that year, but no one made fun of her."

Naomi's domestic scene was none too smooth a sea at that time. Everything was in flux because her boyfriend Larry Strickland and his band were on the road a great deal of the time. It took a lot of dates to keep a ten-man band afloat. Stories of road whores and wild parties after the show are as old as the entertainment industry itself, and Naomi was fiercely jealous.

"She was very jealous that he might be out there gettin' it on," said Joe Sun, a talented singer whose signature hit is "Old Flames (Can't Hold a Candle to You)." "Guys in the band used to tell me that she'd drive all over hell and back to spy on him, to see if he had girls on the road. They'd look down a dark street somewhere, like Boston or somewhere, and there'd be that car parked in the shadow of a building with Naomi sittin' in the dark watching them load onto the bus and drive off."

As that year ground to a close, Christmas loomed as a bittersweet season at the Judds' Franklin farmhouse. Naomi was surrounded by the music business and had found good friends who were part of it, even if she was still vying for her own place among them. But there was something missing: Polly. Christmas was a family thing for the Judds. They made their lye soap for unforgettable gifts, decorated the house colorfully, and looked forward to a candlelight church service on Christmas eve. But memories of Ashland, and her continuing estrangement from her mother touched Naomi with sadness when they sang "Silent Night." Judd women were a stubborn lot. Neither was willing to make the first move toward rapprochement.

"There was something wrong," Naomi recalled sadly. "The whole time she knew it; I knew it. The kids suffered; everybody suffered. I remember the first time I saw Mom after the separation. There just aren't words to describe it. It was like 'Okay, I'm a whole person again.' It was almost like going through another divorce."

As the new year rolled into January, Naomi turned thirty-five with a renewed sense of purpose. Wynonna was so addicted to music that it was obvious that nothing else would suit her. She hadn't paid enough attention to school the last four years to come out prepared for college, yet she lacked the maturity and sense to pursue a serious career for herself.

"She was double promoted in grade school, but when she was eleven and found music, she traded her books for a guitar," Naomi confessed. "The teachers all loved her, but they told me she was a dreamer. She would sit and stare out a window or draw or eat or read a magazine. I pulled my hair out."

Wynonna's talent was surely up to it, and she had neglected her studies enough that her mother knew that she had no real future otherwise, so music was going to be their course. Naomi might fail to fly, but no one could accuse her of low aim.

"Whenever Wynonna ever mentioned a career she never talked about getting her own place or going to college or anything," Naomi said. "She was approaching high-school graduation, and I guess that's when it dawned on us that we were going to pursue it."

Wynonna, for all her compulsiveness about music, was too young to appreciate the meaning of her vocal potential. That made Naomi's job even more difficult.

"I knew I wanted to do music," Wynonna asserted. "I knew I didn't want to go to college . . . But if you'd sat me down and said we'd be big stars and everything would happen like this, I'd have laughed, walked off, and said 'dream on.'"

Though Naomi had hitched her own star to her daughter's talent by moving to Nashville in the first place, the onus of responsibility for her daughter, combined with the natural competition that often exists between mothers and oldest daughters, was beginning to rub Naomi the wrong way. They had always butted heads in that competition of wills. Wynonna was a dreamy, emotional woman-child, whereas Naomi was quite the obsessive dramatizer, impatient to make her dreams into her reality and equally impatient at having a nearly grown daughter who still expected mama to carry the whole load of their daily living. With all her strict upbringing, Naomi had been unable to instill responsibility in Wynonna.

"She had no interest in anything but music," Naomi recalled. "I would come home so tired from working . . . all day, and there would still be dishes in the sink and washing on the line and she'd be listening to the radio. I thought at one time that one of us was not going to make it out alive."

Two and a half years of dedicated immersion in the music business had netted Naomi a lot of good friends, among them some very talented musicians and songwriters. Though no one knew then, the Judds were on the verge of being discovered by people who could get their careers on track. There are almost always two or three exceptional voices floating around Nashville that, if hooked up with the right combination of producer, musical direction, and songs, could take off like a rocket up the charts.

Finding the right song is arguably the most important key. Owen Bradley recorded Patsy Cline for four years before "Walkin' after Midnight" lifted that incredible voice above the crowd. Cline languished precisely because Bill McCall, the man who had her under long-term contract, had chained his second-rate song catalog to her, not allowing Bradley to look for better material from other writers or publishers. Patsy Cline could never really break through until that contract ran out and she was free to sign directly with Bradley at Decca Records. Then he was free to tap "Crazy" and "I Fall to Pieces."

"We used the exact same studio and players and equipment to make the bombs that we did to make the hits," Bradley said of Cline. "You know, it's like the girl in the tight

Naomi and Louise Mandrell compare notes on being from musical families. *(Alan Mayor)*

As guests on Ralph Emery's cable program "Nashville Now," Naomi reminds Emery that when the Judds first performed on his early-morning farm report, he couldn't remember their names, usually introducing them as the Soap Sisters. *(Melodie Gimple)*

Naomi admires Wynonna's talent on the guitar. *(Dave Findley)*

Naomi's flirtatious stage antics are often aimed at the boys in her band.
(Bill Thorup)

The Judds take home trophies from every awards show they attend. *(Steve Granitz/Celebrity Photo)*

Songwriter Harlan Howard greets Naomi backstage. *(Beth Gwinn)*

The Judds, Conway Twitty, BMI president Frances Preston, and Reba McEntire were on hand for the presentation of a commemorative silver platter to Harlan Howard. Songs written by Howard for all three acts were high in the *Billboard* country charts that week. *(Beth Gwinn)*

The Judds double-team producer Brent Maher. *(Alan Mayor)*

Brent Maher, Wynonna, Naomi, and Don Potter relax at Creative Workshop Studios where they record. *(Alan Mayor)*

sweater: if you don't put something in there—if you don't have a good song then you don't get anything out."

Tight sweaters were never a problem, but the same impediment that bedeviled Patsy Cline's early career would inevitably have held back Naomi's promotion of the Judds. They needed a great song, and Naomi was not writing any. Luckily, a casual friendship with songwriter Kenny O'Dell provided the Judds with what would become their first number 1 hit fully a year before they even had a record deal.

O'Dell had been approached by Naomi for help. She had a pretty clear idea in her own head about what the Judds' sound should be. The problem was, she wasn't experienced enough as a songwriter to compose material for them. The sound that Naomi correctly had in mind for them was complex. It was a mixture of old-timey traditional country harmonies jammed together with the jazzy lines of big-band trios like the Andrews Sisters and the ultrasophisticated harmonies of the Sons of the Pioneers. Thrown in were eclectic and almost inimitable influences from rock and blues, and modal extrapolations from such one-of-a-kind contemporary acts as Warren Zevon, Bonnie Raitt, and Joni Mitchell. The off-the-rack country tune available from Nashville's hit mills tend to be generic waltzes and 4/4 numbers of all tempos, built around as few major chords as possible so that any pickup bar band can easily learn them to front the journeyman recording artist on the club circuit. The Judds, as unique as their sound was, needed songs that were just as unusual. They needed songs that addressed the home-fried values and mother-daughter goodness themes that Naomi had already isolated as their most salable image. What they needed even more was a top-notch songwriter to craft a tune especially for them, and that's what Naomi got from O'Dell.

"At that time, I was trying to help Naomi get her songs together as a songwriter," O'Dell explained. "The two of them, the ideas they had were semideveloped and they sounded real good, but never quite came together."

Prompted by the dramatic stories that Naomi had told him about their lives, O'Dell lifted an idea from a daytime soap opera and began writing a song just for them. O'Dell had produced some of his own earlier attempts at a pop-artist career, such as "(You Just Gotta Be One of the Most) Beautiful People." In meetings to discuss a possible production deal with him, Naomi and Wynonna sang Naomi's "Lazy Country Evenings" and "My Mama Says." With these two songs to guide him stylistically and thematically, O'Dell's prodigious talents could not fail to deliver. When he brought his new song "Mama He's Crazy" to Naomi early in 1982, Naomi knew that the key piece in the Judds creative concept was in place. Anyone to whom they presented themselves from then on would hear that song and would hear the definition of Naomi's dream.

There was still the matter of finding someone like Shulenberger again, someone willing to gamble his own money and talents on them. It wasn't going to be easy. First, Naomi was demanding control of any situation, girded by the belief that a mother-daughter duo singing about the homey middle-American values of faithful love and dreams come true was the ticket. She felt that that image reflected their inner selves. Any professional who might want to work with them would have to accept the ultimate direction of Naomi.

"I've gone by my own gut instinct all my life," she explained.

As the Sound Shop sessions had proved to her, compromising her vision of the Judds as both a creative and a marketable duo package made things happen quicker, but not the right things.

Wynonna has called her "the neurotic, dramatic Naomi of the universe," referring to both her driving ambitions and

her behavioral style. Naive as she was about the machina-
tions, if not the personalities, of the country-music business,
Naomi was going to be *the* force to deal with for any manager, publicist, or producer willing to take a risk on them.
Few would-be artists have that kind of vision of themselves or
the all-or-nothing resolve to insist on it. Naomi Judd just
didn't know her limits. Had she even suspected she had limits, she would never have let that stop her from trying anyway. She didn't know specifically who or what they needed,
but she was certain that she'd know it when she found it.

"I was looking for a producer who could develop the
unique sound that we had in our hearts and minds, not to
mention someone who I could leave my daughter alone in
the room with," Naomi explained. "We were determined to
keep control of the situation, as far as maintaining the integ-
rity of our music. We wanted to make sure that nobody
messed with our sound. We needed somebody who realized
that our voices were the main instruments and that all the
rest was just decoration."

It was quite a radical change from the shy, less than self-
confident seventeen-year-old Diana who had crumpled into
the arms of the rich boy from across town as an escape from
the end of childhood's dreams.

If their mother-daughter fights got worse as Wynonna
approached graduation from Franklin High, their mother-
daughter harmonies only got better. Naomi stood proudly at
the back of the auditorium as Wynonna and a musician from
the band Memphis performed at the school's talent contest.
Their segment came as the judges tallied up the scores on the
students in competition. Already seen as a pro, she wasn't in
the running for a ten-dollar prize and a blue ribbon. Her
sights were set higher. She had been voted Most Talented as
a senior superlative, posing in a matronly outfit for the portrait that made her look like the cartoon character Nancy's

frumpy Aunt Fritzy. On the other hand, her actual senior picture (taken by a portrait photographer) was quite a dreamy and sophisticated image of sex appeal, rather than the stock head and shoulders shot taken by the official school photographer. Naomi, as always the director of such things, was still trying on image poses for her daughter.

Throughout her years in Nashville, Naomi had worked mainly as a nurse, part of that time as a roving substitute and part at Williamson County Hospital in Franklin. She spent as much time away from that job as possible, expecting to make the inevitable connection down on Music Row. Ironically, one of the most important connections that she would ever make came in through the emergency-room doors while she was on duty.

One night, near Franklin High School graduation day, a friend of Wynonna's was in a bad car wreck. Diana Maher was hurt badly enough to require a lengthy stay at Williamson County Hospital. Luckily for the Judds, she wound up on Naomi's floor. In telling Wynonna about the girl, Naomi found out that Wynonna knew Diana, and learned that the girl's father was a bubbling-under producer—a man with talent, but with a middling track record for producing cuts on Kenny Rogers's albums and a couple of hit records for Dottie West.

"I was working as a full-time registered nurse at Williamson County Hospital, and Wynonna was in high school," Naomi recalled. "The hospital admitted this girl who had been in a car wreck. I later found out her father was a big-time Nashville producer."

Brent Maher was his name. Naomi checked out some of his production credits. He had some good ones, if he hadn't yet broken out of the pack with either a monster hit or a new artist. What she didn't find out was that Maher had worked in the Las Vegas studio with Kenny O'Dell years earlier and with a certain quirky guitarist named Don Potter in New York in the midseventies. Maher was the one man who would understand the creative direction that she felt in her gut but didn't have the background or experience to create or articulate. She committed that name to memory.

Without the money to invest in studio time, Naomi and Wynonna tested harmony ideas that were now growing beyond what they could do with their two voices alone. With the Sons of the Pioneers and the Andrews Sisters as sources, they were pulling up some exciting sounds. They worked "Mama He's Crazy" into a state of vocal perfection with the aid of some very low-tech recorders.

"We became fascinated with some unusual variations that you can get with four-part harmonies," Wynonna remembered. "So we went out and bought these two thirty-dollar blue-light special tape recorders from K-Mart. We'd sing our duets into one tape recorder, then play it back and sing harmonies against ourselves into the other recorder."

When Diana Maher was getting ready to leave the hospital, she suggested that Naomi give her a tape that she could carry to her father. She had recognized Wynonna's talent the year before but could never get her father interested. Naomi gave her that "funky little homemade tape," which promptly got lost in a slush pile of demos her father carried around in the front seat of his car as something to listen to as he drove home each night from the studio where he worked. Maher's wife had awakened him before dawn a couple of mornings during the preceding year so that he could see the Soap Sisters on Ralph Emery's show as well, but they still hadn't gotten his attention.

"My wife would see these girls on 'The Ralph Emery Show' and shake me out of bed at six o'clock in the morning to come and look at them," Maher said. "I kept saying, 'They sure are pretty and they sure can sing good,' and then go back to bed."

Naomi was willing to let her fate ride for a few weeks on the uncertainty that Diana Maher could get her father to screen their homemade demo before she decided to pursue it in person. In the meantime, she kept her eye out for a manager. As Jon Shulenberger had discovered, Naomi's idea of a manager was that of a road manager. She knew plenty of those: guys who took care of all the logistical details of a touring country band, checked them into hotels, made sure the equipment arrived and got set up on time—made sure that the twenty-two hours of hard work that happens before a two-hour concert got done. If Naomi wasn't really sure what a manager's role was, she knew that every working act had at least one.

The minimum requirement of a career manager is that he or she know a lot of important people and have their confidence, if not their overt friendship. It helps immeasurably if the manager has a big pile of money; even more if he or she understands how the music business works from top to bottom, to be able to make the right moves at the right time and keep his or her client from getting shorted in negotiations.

When she didn't hear back from Maher soon enough to suit her, Naomi followed up on her own.

"On my day off I got dressed up and went to his studio," she explained. "I said 'Remember me, the one who brought your daughter her pain shots on time?' I gave him a tape of the two of us, just the two voices and guitar. Some of it was songs I had written, plus a medley of our eclectic tastes."

He didn't play the tape right away, but its placement in his front-seat slush pile with the other one gave her double the chance of getting heard. It was only a matter of time before his hand came up with the Judds' homemade demo as

he drove home previewing material and new acts on his car
stereo.

Key players in the Judds' eventual rise to stardom began
falling into place right after Wynonna's eighteenth birthday
and her high-school graduation. It was as if her reaching the
age of majority had removed the lock from the door to opportunity for them. Ricky Skaggs had broken through to his first
gold record in the preceding year and a half, but he hadn't
forgotten the girls from around his hometown—not that
Naomi would have let him. When he was scheduled to perform for some fifteen thousand fans at International Fan Fair
early in the summer of 1982, he provided Naomi with a
special backstage pass for the CBS Records Show and invited
her to join him there.

Skaggs introduced Naomi to his own independent publicist, Woody Bowles. Skaggs recommended Naomi and Wynonna to Bowles as a talented pair that bore watching, but
Bowles's immediate reaction was one of tepid politeness.
Bowles knew that people without records didn't need publicity. Newly married, Bowles was keeping his mind on business
that promised to pay him for his time. Naomi looked more
like trouble than business on first impression. She decided to
follow up that introduction anyway.

Bowles had an "off-campus" office about a mile from
Music Row. The nicest thing was that it had three rooms: the
more doors people have to go through to get to a music-
industry executive, the more important he appears to be.
Bowles's receptionist will probably never forget the day that
Naomi dragged her quiet daughter and her big blond guitar
into Bowles's outer office, insisting in the most classic of ruses
that she had an appointment. At length, when the Judds
wouldn't go away, Bowles shuffled his work schedule and

agreed to let them in for a brief meeting. An hour later Naomi was still talking.

Anyone who has had the baffling pleasure of being caught in the cross fire of a conversation with Naomi and Wynonna Judd might understand the mixture of fascination and frustration that must have filled Bowles when he finally stopped the meeting and asked the $64,000 question: "Can you girls sing?"

Wynonna pulled out her guitar, and they proceeded to absolutely shatter Bowles's cynical defenses. The years of singing for fun around the kitchen table came to a head right there in his office, and Bowles was impressed. More than that, he had goose bumps. In the following months, as he told his friends in the business about his discovery he would shake his head and smile when he countered skepticism at their homely names, saying, "You're not going to believe these girls!"

Bowles wanted to trust his intuition, his goose bumps, but he was pretty far out on a limb considering Naomi's offer to let him manage them. She had mentioned something about Brent Maher, of whom Bowles knew. When he called Maher to confer with him, he found that the producer had just listened to Naomi's tape a few days before and had nearly driven his Mercedes off the road in surprise. They talked each other into accepting the Judds as clients. Now the ball was rolling.

"Well, we got lucky," Naomi explained. "Maher put the tape on [as he was] driving, and he laughed because we were so off-the-wall. He came by to visit, and we started singing—bluegrass, big band, country."

"What planet are you from?" Naomi said Maher had asked her.

"This is Judd music," Wynonna answered. "Brent Maher opened the door for us, and it really changed our lives."

The first noticeable change was in the number of new faces at the after-dinner guitar pulls in the Judds' kitchen. Maher began dropping over regularly, bringing songwriters and occasionally a musician that he thought might hook into what these women were all about. Shulenberger had found out the hard way that their sound just could not be captured by any off-the-rack studio rhythm section. They were special and more than a little quirky.

"Well, he listened to our tape, contacted us, and started coming by our farm on his way home from the studio," Naomi said. "He would work with us a lot in the evening . . . Then later he'd come by our house in the evening and we'd sing for him. It amazed him to hear everything we used to sing. One night we would sing southern gospel, and the next night some boogie-woogie. Or maybe we would sing the blues by Delbert McClinton or Bonnie Raitt."

Another key player was a New York refugee, guitarist Don Potter, a man who then suspected that he might well be at the end of his commercial music career.

"[Maher] brought over Don Potter," Wynonna said. "So we worked with Don for a good four or five months. One minute we'd sing like the Andrews Sisters, and the next I'd sing him something by Bonnie Raitt. We worked and worked, and we sat around every day at the supper table until we finally got what we wanted."

In 1982 Potter was, thanks to Maher's encouragement, just coming out of a weird period in his life during which he had laid down his guitar because it scared him. He had experienced a deep religious conversion, and Maher had convinced him that his talent shouldn't be hidden under a bushel. If the Lord was the most important thing to him, he should use his music to praise him, like the children's hymn "This Little Light of Mine" says. Once Potter had made the commitment to return to his music, the step to working with the Judds was relatively easy and fortuitous for all concerned.

"He came to dinner, and we started singing," Wynonna explained. "By the time he left, I felt I had known him all my life. He's been with us on all our albums. I've never met a more gentle-spirited soul than Don."

Potter remembers their first meeting even more vividly.

"The first time I sat in their living room and heard them sing 'John Deere Tractor'—which was the first song I heard them sing—every hair on my body stood up on end," Potter told Chicago *Tribune* music writer Jack Hurst. "I looked at those two girls and said to myself there was no way they wouldn't be number-1 stars. Their music was just too strong."

Potter is an interesting story in himself.

Born in Glens Falls, New York, Potter was more fumbled than handed off between his divorced and oft-remarried mother and father. The only time he attended church during his unstable childhood was when he lived with his grand-mother. Potter found himself living in California by his twelfth birthday. There, at about the same age at which Wynonna Judd began playing, he discovered the guitar. As with Wynonna, the guitar became Potter's best friend and music his emotional refuge as he was uprooted time and again.

After a few more years, Don had seen enough of both parents. He forged his father's name to a car note when he turned fifteen and ran away from home. He got a job at a gas station to pay for the car. Potter couldn't afford an apartment on his short paycheck, so he set up housekeeping in the backseat of his car, where he whiled away his off-hours prac-ticing his guitar. Wynonna might have regarded it as an inno-cent prank back on Bighill when she swiped her mother's cookie-jar money for new guitar strings, but Potter had to consciously choose between a meal and a set of silk and steels.

A guy can always eat tomorrow, but no one can fret a G-major 7th diminished with a broken B string.

Potter eventually wandered back to upstate New York. There he combined talents with another musician and eventually earned a recording contract with Epic Records as a duo. A Nashville-connected producer was involved in the album, which led nowhere in the short run but would eventually lead Potter to Tennessee looking for that producer again. In the meantime, he opened a coffeehouse, where his playing attracted a variety of New York–based professionals. He was discovered there by popular jazz player Chuck Mangione and invited to play concerts with him regularly. From the early sixties, for about ten years Potter was part of the larger Mangione touring band. He based himself at his coffeehouse and in his duo when Mangione went out with his quartet.

In 1973, when his second coffeehouse and the duo had both gone bust, Potter moved to Nashville, where he drew the interest of CBS Records producer Billy Sherrill, whose production credits included Tammy Wynette and George Jones. Sherrill produced three singles for Potter as a singer, but the R & B sound was too black for country radio and too white for R & B stations. His records had some success on easy-listening charts, but his best ideas wound up being lifted for another CBS artist with better credentials, leaving him in the position of sounding like an imitator of the act who had ripped off his own sound. Friends report that Potter got kind of crazy about that time.

Indeed, with the Mangione job behind him and his own recording career snuffed by intracorporate politics, sources report that he started drinking heavily. He eventually returned to New York, where he played sessions and clubs, falling into what he called "a pretty easy life, musically."

Easy guitar gigs didn't make his inner life more comfortable, however. Bored, mentally exhausted, and with his marriage in poor condition, Potter essentially snapped his elastic in the late seventies. He began searching in Eastern religions for relief from his pain and bewilderment. When he found Jesus, he gave up his guitar.

"My wife and I accepted the Lord in 1981," he explained. "I had to lay music down because I had made it too much of a god in my life. Music had caused me to be insensitive to everybody, especially my wife."

Walking away from a comfortable but stymied career, he returned to Nashville, thinking that there might be a place for him in the music business. He was easily turned away from it, though, because his heart was no longer in it. He joined a nondenominational congregation called the House of Blessing and turned his talented hands to hammer and nails as a carpenter, having picked up knowledge of the construction trade, just as he had music, from his itinerant father.

Brent Maher saw just how unique Potter's talent was and encouraged him to pick it up again.

"[Maher] had bought his son a guitar and asked me to check it out," Potter explained. "I started tinkering around with it, and he got this look on his face. He said, 'Boy, I need to do something with you in the studio.' "

Maher would deliver the opportunity for Potter to record an instrumental album, *Free Yourself,* in 1984, for Myrrh Records, the religious publishing and record label of Word, Inc. But first, there was a little matter of a new mother and daughter duo he had discovered.

"What Brent had in mind [in recording the Judds] was to get your hair standing on end when you listened to the record, exactly the way mine did when I first heard them in their living room," Potter explained.

It would be Potter's job to help find the right musical accompaniment to help Naomi and Wynonna do just that, whenever the Judds' management team managed to obtain a recording contract.

T·E·N

Pulling Together, Flying Apart

Maher, Potter, Wynonna, and Naomi needed only guitars and a kitchen table to begin their work together. Manager Woody Bowles had bigger problems. He needed a lot of money, and quickly. No bank would loan cash for such a risky venture. Bowles was already managing the musical-comedy team of Sandy Pinkard and Richard Bowden, and it was stretching his resources. Pinkard and Bowden had just gotten a record deal with Warner Bros. and were making a name for themselves writing parodies of well-known hit songs. Physically, they are the Laurel and Hardy of musical comedy, dressed in 1930s-style cowboy business suits and twenty-gallon Stetson hats. The Judds weren't a self-contained act like Pinkard and Bowden; they were going to be expensive.

Bowles soon realized that he would need a partner to bankroll the management company that he was forming within his public-relations office. He knew that the business had more sharks than fairy godmothers hanging around; he just hoped that he could find a partner who wouldn't muscle him out of the picture as soon as the Judds were a happening thing.

When the major labels passed on Wynonna, Shulenberger had presented her to small independent record companies, but even they had turned the act down. One of those who discounted Wynonna as a solo was now interested in the Judds as a mother-daughter duo. Bowles approached Dimension Records owner Ken Stilts and caught his ear with a tape. Stilts had made his money in industrial manufacturing, in partnership with a brother in S & S Industries. With factories in four states, they had made a killing during the latter half of the 1970s during the energy crunch by making wraparound insulation for water heaters.

From his main factory in Hendersonville, Tennessee, Stilts had matriculated around the fringes of the country-music business. The Oak Ridge Boys' offices and recording studio was there, as was Johnny Cash's House of Cash operations and museum. As early as the late seventies, Conway Twitty was circulating plans for a mammoth live-in tourist attraction. He eventually convinced the Hendersonville city government to underwrite it with a bond issue. It's called Twitty City. Also, a number of sleazy fringe operators based their fly-by-night record companies in huge warehouse-style buildings, holding lavish parties until the appropriate law enforcement agencies found the holes in their tax-loss schemes or caught them pressing records they didn't own. It was all pretty exciting to Stilts, who found new bundles of cash rolling in every time OPEC raised the price of oil another dollar.

Stilts entered the country-music business in a serious way when he signed Louisiana songwriter Eddy Raven to a management contract. When he couldn't get Raven a deal at an established record label, he formed his own: Dimension Records. Eventually, counting on Raven's songwriting abilities to generate a hit record, Dimension managed to get "Dealing with That Devil" up into the *Billboard* Top 20 country singles chart. At that point Stilts was able to get a contract for Raven with his golfing buddy Jimmy Bowen, who directed Elektra Records' country division in Nashville. Raven's career stalled at Elektra. He later cut a deal with RCA and severed relations with Stilts, but Stilts had certainly demonstrated that he had the money it took to promote talent in the pantheon of country stars.

Stilts and Bowles became partners in the Judds' management. Sandy Pinkard gave some insights into those early weeks of the Ken Stilts–Woody Bowles management effort to build the Judds and themselves.

"I remember the day they came in there and sang for him. They were just real cute and fresh," Pinkard recalled. "The first time I ever met Naomi, she showed up at Close Quarters [a popular late-night hangout for people in the music business] in her nursing outfit. It was late at night, the lights were low, and boy, don't you think in an all white outfit like that that she didn't stand out. Everything was like that, everything was really calculated. They were a little exposed in those early days. . . . See, Ken had made his money in gaskets—S & S Industries—then when they had the first bad energy crisis they slapped together Styrofoam jackets for water heaters. His concept of management is 'pilemanship': he has a pile here and a pile there. It ain't like he's the president's economic adviser."

But you can afford to make a lot of minor mistakes when you have enough money behind you to correct them, and that was Stilts's strong suit. Bowles's job was to try to interest an established label. That would take time and many failed attempts. But Stilts and Bowles were certain that the Judds' talent was unique, and that Maher and Potter were good enough at what they were doing that it would all fall into place—eventually. In the meantime, Naomi and Wynonna were still workaday women.

They suddenly found themselves in an exciting and yet frustrating world of competing realities. On the one hand, they had a sensitive producer and an empathetic guitarist working with them several nights a week polishing their music. They had a pair of solicitous managers swarming over them, conferring on career development plans and encouraging them. On the other hand, Naomi still had to put on her nurse's uniform most days and go to the hospital, where there were temperatures to be taken, medicines to administer, and bed pans to empty.

She had pushed Wynonna out into the world of work after high school. Local temporary-labor agencies assigned her to a series of receptionist and secretarial jobs around Nashville. Driven by her obsessions and not the least interested in anything but her music, Wynonna hated secretarial work and made no bones about it. Swinging between being on the verge of glamour and the nine-to-five realities of work and small paychecks, the Judds' world was a topsy-turvy seesaw through the winter of 1982–83. Younger daughter Ashley was a sophomore at Franklin High, no longer a cheerleader, but carving her own niche outside the whirlwind of music that had commandeered her home. At least everyone said that they were spinning upward for a change.

Don Potter and Brent Maher experimented to find just the right approach for surrounding Naomi and Wynonna's voices with music. Potter, who was already deeply involved with his religion, struck a similar chord in Naomi, who harbored ingrained faith from her mother's Sunday-school lessons. They got along famously. For Potter, playing with the Judds was similar to his charismatic religious experience, in that it was highly emotional and deeply satisfying. Naomi allowed and sometimes encouraged him to share that perspective with her for the comfort it provided in the face of the pressures of approaching success. As they came closer to perfecting each tune in their repertoire, these already emotional people were suffused with a natural high. That was exactly what producer Maher wanted to re-create in their music.

As they got ready to take the Judds into Maher's favorite studio, the concept of an all-acoustic instrumentation emerged from the unbeatable feel of their demo tapes.

"The first time we'd go through each song to get ready for the master sessions, we'd do it with just Wynonna and me playing acoustic and Brent slapping his leg or something," Potter told the Chicago *Tribune*'s Jack Hurst. "And as we'd have little ideas, I'd express each idea on the acoustic guitar, and we'd put it on the demo of the song so we could always remember what the idea was. We just got so used to hearing the acoustic guitar playing those ideas that it became part of their sound. It wasn't me. I call it one of those divine accidents."

Woody Bowles, striving to find a record label for the act, ran into brick walls at first. The confusing impression made by quiet Wynonna and flashy Naomi during Jon Shulenberger's interviews with label heads had muddied the waters for him on Music Row. There was some discussion of reviving Dimension Records, but Stilts knew from bitter experience just how difficult it was to recoup a career-building investment on a manager's percentage, and this time he was splitting the cut with Bowles. The total investment to push the Judds from ground zero to their first full-length RIAA-certified gold record—including the record company's large share—might be as high as one million dollars. Bowles kept trying.

Eventually, Bowles decided that he had struck out on Music Row. Unless he and Stilts could find a stronger partner, one with the clout to get the duo seriously considered at a major Nashville label, they might just as well write off their time and money. They were sunk. Bowles took a chance and sent a rough demo tape of the Judds to Dick Whitehouse, head of Curb Records in California. Curb is a strong middleman operation, signing acts and then cutting deals with major labels. Among the country artists who are currently listed on the Curb–other company dual label are Hank Williams, Jr. (Curb/Warner) and the Bellamy Brothers (MCA/Curb). It was a good move, and it paid off. Bowles arranged for Naomi and Wynonna to meet Whitehouse the next time he was in Nashville and give him a private concert. He signed them right away.

"We did a little audition for him in a hotel room," Wynonna explained. "Then he, Woody Bowles, and Ken Stilts, along with Brent, went to RCA."

They were on the brink of their big break.

"So, at 6 P.M., March 2, 1983, we walked into Joe Galante's office in single file with a guitar and played 'A Mother's Smile,'" Wynonna said. "They told us to wear our best dresses. It was very spontaneous. We didn't have anything lined up. We just did what we felt."

For a heady forty-five minutes, Naomi and Wynonna poured out their souls to Galante and his immediate associates, singing anything that came to mind. Don Potter sat quietly in the corner, playing when needed and saying nothing. Galante asked some questions and got treated to that cute, quirky mother-daughter cross fire for answers. What they were doing was extremely rare in the new Nashville. They had always wound up on a couch in someone's office (or in Dick Whitehouse's case, in a hotel suite) singing their auditions, but by the time important people got as close to a serious decision as Joe Galante was at that moment, the bait was more typically a twenty-four-track master recording, a much slicker presentation than the Judds had made. If Naomi had only known just how unusual this opportunity was, she might have been too nervous to sing.

"We really didn't know any better," she explained. "I think if it hadn't been for the fact that we rely so heavily on the voices and guitar, then we might have had to go into a studio and do a production tape. But we did about six or seven songs, told them our story, and they're looking around the room at each other like, 'Oh yeah, sure.' "

"They were expecting country, and of course we are country, but I don't think they were ready for us," Wynonna said.

All too soon, the audition was over. Galante had seen enough. Now there was some high-level talking to do with Dick Whitehouse. The Judds and Maher were ushered out, with the promising admonition that they should not go too far.

"Mom and I kind of curtsied and went out the door," Wynonna recalled. "Brent took us down the street to a restaurant where we waited for about the longest hour of my life."

They adjourned to Maude's, a favorite meeting place for people in the music business, whether they're famous or the folks in the back office. It is a place to see and be seen, a place to go when you are happening, not a hangout for losers. Wynonna wadded napkins, while Naomi tried to keep the atmosphere light by turning on her zany sense of humor. The jury was out for little more than an hour; then Dick Whitehouse suddenly appeared at their table. The look on his face told them all that they needed to know. RCA was going to offer a deal. The celebration started right away.

For that one brief evening, all the pressure was off. They had made it. The story is told on Nashville's Music Row that when she got the contract offer from RCA Records, Naomi held up the deal trying to get unrealistic concessions.

Percentage points, reserves against returns, cross-collateralized recoupment of costs—none of these details of major-label contract negotiations meant anything to Naomi when it came time to cut her own record deal. Yet she knew by heart the price of tour-bus tires and how often they had to be rotated and replaced. What she wanted most from RCA was a customized Silver Eagle tour bus, the fat-cat El Dorado of country-music transportation. All her favorite stars had them, and she just assumed that the record companies provided them to their stars. She was wrong, but that had never stopped her before.

Nearly everything Naomi Judd knew about the professional end of the country-music business had come from her boyfriend, the idle conversations of bar bands, and fan magazines. She was ill equipped for detailed contract negotiating, but she wasn't the kind to just sit back and let other people handle it all when she had specific expectations. She had dated a number of musicians, songwriters, and publishers, but few "stars." All she knew about life on the road with a country band was to be green-eyed jealous of her main boyfriend. Having had an early, if brief, career in the back office of the entertainment industry as receptionist for the Fifth Dimension, she had learned what she could about the business, but that involved small club bands floating ninety-day notes for their PA system, hoping for the big break that never came.

Now, the Judds' big break had come. Ambitious and nobody's fool, Naomi grabbed hold of this, the opportunity she had pushed, planned, and angled toward for the previous six years. She would make over herself and her tremendously talented but dangerously moody eldest daughter—even if it killed both of them.

Naomi and Wynonna giggled and whooped like lottery winners when they were told of RCA's offer. When they signed with RCA they were charismatic, engaging amateurs who talked a mile a minute simultaneously to anyone who would listen, and they fought like a stubborn mother and a willful daughter in front of everyone. They would become polished concert professionals and Naomi would get them that big old Silver Eagle if it hair-lipped the stone heads on Mount Rushmore. It wouldn't be easy, but then neither had much of anything else on her amazing, cross-country odyssey to get out front and shine.

But no sooner did the ink dry on their recording contract than the serious frictions that had been building between Naomi and her half-woman, half-child daughter began to really throw sparks. They were expected to begin recording a six-song mini-album for RCA right away. The decision was made to send them out with Don Potter to visit radio stations and do the same kind of face-to-face promotion that stressed their natural charm. Life was getting hectic.

Stilts tried to give them some breathing room away from each other at least five days a week by encouraging them to keep their day jobs. It helped a little, but not enough. Suddenly, Naomi began demanding that Wynonna shape up to a new set of standards. She had always browbeaten Wynonna about her weight problem, but now it got worse. Not only was Wynonna nagged about keeping her room clean and helping out around the house; she was now expected to suddenly change overnight and begin to act like an adult and a business professional. Wynonna was simply unequipped emotionally to do all that, much less accept her mother's dramatic style of insistence. She was at the natural age of rebellion anyway; she resented Naomi's nagging, and she wore her emotions on her sleeve. Naomi was much too authoritarian to coolly manipulate things into place. She wanted Wynonna, eighteen and quite bullheaded in her own right, to straighten up and fly right. Wynonna would fly all right, fly right out of the house and maybe out of the deal.

"I was a little unsure, you know," Wynonna said later, drastically understating the situation. "Between seventeen and nineteen I went through that rebellious stage of wanting to know everything on my own, and when we got signed by RCA and decided to go on the road and everything, it was almost like tying two cats' tails together and throwing them over a clothesline. We weren't sure. I'll be honest with you, we didn't know what might happen."

Rolling Stone magazine reported on the next thing that happened. Wynonna and Naomi reached the point where they fought so viciously and came so close to violence with each other that Naomi threw her oldest daughter out of the house. It is hard enough for a mother to adjust to a first daughter reaching the age of majority, but the natural competition that exists between a mother and an oldest daughter grew out of all proportion. A mother cat will walk away from her kittens to keep them off her when it's time to wean them, but she will still clean and groom them lovingly. The suddenness of the Judds' impending shot at stardom accelerated what should have been a slower and less traumatic process into an instant crisis. Neither of them had the foresight to suggest that Wynonna simply needed to get out from under Naomi's roof before they killed each other.

"Coming as it did right after high school, I didn't have a chance to move out of the house, become responsible, and make mistakes," Wynonna explained. "I had to make them in front of her."

"And of course, a mother sees any mistakes the child makes as a reflection on her parenting," Naomi added. "So I was under a lot of pressure."

Life got crazy for the responsible parties around them.

Rehearsing new songs or working on demo tapes with Potter and Maher seemed to be the only place where they could suspend their animosity and cooperate. As with their earlier experience in Morrill, they clung to each other when they were making music. Otherwise, they were in a nearly-constant state of competition and acrimony. It was something their managers didn't want RCA to see. They had bought into an image of loving mother-daughter harmonies, the good life of honest values and all that happily-ever-after stuff. Stilts and Bowles tried their best to keep them in line, or at least to keep their conflicts away from RCA ears, but it finally blew up in their faces when Naomi threw Wynonna out of the house in a fit of frustration and anger. Wynonna knew where she could find a friend, and she needed one badly right then. She left Nashville for Ocala, Florida, where Michael Ciminella offered to let her live with him as long as she needed to while she cleared her head and decided what she really wanted to do with her life. According to *Rolling Stone,* she considered ending it one night soon after arriving in Florida. She had had a few drinks and was out in her father's car, driving fast down a lonesome road. At one hundred miles per hour, it would be so easy just to turn the wheel into the ditch . . .

"That comes with the confusion [of being] an adolescent, a young woman who is told by a lot of people that she can, if she wants to, become a big success and control her own destiny," Ciminella explained. "[Suicide] was just one of a lot of options that ran through her mind at the time when she was staying with me [in Florida], but as far as actually loading a gun and doing something like that, I don't think it ever really got as far as that.

"More of Christina's attitude at that time could be summed up by 'Sweet Bird of Youth.' She was concerned about what to do with herself, whether to pursue a career in

Manager Ken Stilts holds the umbrella for Wynonna as they played in the rain for their 1985 homecoming charity concert in Ashland. *(Jim Donithan/Ashland Daily Independent)*

The Judds were made honorary Kentucky Colonels before their benefit show for King's Daughters' Medical Center. *(Jim Donithan/Ashland Daily Independent)*

Performing is the biggest thrill. *(Alan Mayor)*

The Judds display their 1985 Hat Award from the Academy of Country
Music. *(Beth Gwinn)*

Wynonna's sexy smile looks more like Elvis Presley's every day. *(John McCormick)*

The Judds enjoy meeting other stars, so Wynonna sometimes takes her autograph book backstage at awards shows. Here they are introduced to pop-gospel headliner Amy Grant. *(Alan Mayor)*

Naomi's younger daughter, Ashley Ciminella, joins her mother and sister in the spotlight on rare occasions. *(Scott Downie/Celebrity Photo)*

"This one's me; I'm the mother," says Naomi after autographing an early publicity photo for a friend. *(Bill Thorup)*

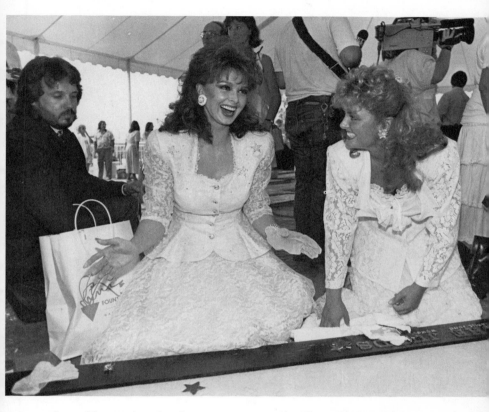

The Judds put their handprints in concrete for the NARAS Grammy
Walkway of Fame in Nashville. *(John Carnes and Associates)*

The Judds and Reba McEntire were a potent box-office draw, touring together often in 1987. *(Bill Thorup)*

the music business and whether she could, or really wanted
to, live with and be involved in a career with her mother on a
long-term basis. She wondered about herself, wondered if
when she got up in front of thousands of people to sing . . .
she would choke up. It was a lot of pressure on a young
woman, an adolescent.

"She was distraught, though. We spent a lot of time on
the back porch discussing all this. Her talent, the options to
do this or not, what a grind it could be spending months and
months on little buses going across the country. But the buses
got big before anyone really expected them to."

After a few weeks, Wynonna made her decision and
returned to Nashville. Still too immature to understand that
it was a mistake, she moved back into her mother's house. No
sooner had Maher breathed a sigh of relief and gone back to
picking songs for the Judds to record than there was another
blowup between Naomi and Wynonna.

"They did a lot of fighting; they fought like cats and dogs
constantly," recalled Sandy Pinkard. "The mother was very
unhappy with the immaturity of the daughter. It just wasn't
happening. You know, Wynonna went and lived with Elaine
and Woody for a while in the middle of all that. They always
fought about little stuff like Wy not cleaning up her space.
They were running into a crunch as far as being around each
other so much. They were all of a sudden having to be around
each other all the time. Such a great amount of energy was
going out on that. Woody and Elaine were having twins right
about then, too, and it was just hard on everybody."

Wynonna had shown up unexpectedly on the Bowles's
door step with a change of clothes and her overnight case.
She had been thrown out again, this time for keeps. Woody
Bowles turned to Ken Stilts and got only a do-what-you-have-
to-do nod, along with the warning that this could sink the
whole deal for everyone if the women couldn't be kept to-

gether at least on the professional level. The simple solution might have been to help Wynonna find an apartment of her own and let it go at that, but Wynonna Judd was too complex a character and too much the goose that was about to lay the golden egg to take that chance. She was too immature to live on her own at just barely eighteen. Everyone, especially Naomi, was afraid of what might happen to her if left to her own devices (of which she really had none). She needed to be looked after, and right in the middle of welcoming their own twin boys into their Brentwood home, the Bowles family welcomed Wynonna.

"I have to admit, it was real strange when it happened," Naomi said. "But we felt for the sanity of the relationship we need what little time we have to ourselves."

Woody Bowles, serving in the unasked-for role of *in loco parentis,* was thus put in the hot seat within the management company. What he had on his hands was a confused eighteen-year-old who had the voice of a seasoned thirty-year-old, the body of an adult woman (albeit plumped with baby fat), and the level of responsibility of a five-year-old. He was responsible for making decisions for Wynonna that would steer the careers of both her and her mother, with the added specter of Naomi's expectation that he keep her little girl out of trouble. Up until August of 1983, that had seemed little problem. Wynonna, addicted to music, funny clothes, and candy bars, had never had a serious boyfriend. She had already passed the age at which her mother's fate was sealed on that account. Many of her girlfriends had gone to college out of town, but those who remained behind noticed a sudden change in Wynonna a couple of months after she got away from her mother's ever-watchful eye and began to come into her own.

"When we were cruising in the neat old Chevy, she would turn the radio way up and sing along real loud. She was good," high-school pal Kim McCarthy recalled. "The three of us would go skating or hang out somewhere. Then she met this boy and we stopped hanging out. She wasn't the kind of girl who had a lot of boys wanting to go out with her in high school. [All of a sudden] she was spending a lot of time on her music, and the rest of the time she spent with her boyfriend."

Wynonna's boyfriend was a lantern-jawed, all-American boy, handsome and sweet to her. As her affection for the boy grew, Wynonna couldn't help sharing the news with her mother.

"Wynonna pulled me aside one evening and said, 'You know that song ["Mama He's Crazy"]? It's come true,'" Naomi said. "We just hugged each other and cried."

To Naomi's everlasting relief, he was not preoccupied with sex. Steve McCord was working as a landscape helper around Franklin that summer when he and Wynonna began spending time together. Wynonna was a babe in the woods when it came to men. She simply had no experience, good or bad. As Naomi confided to her hairdresser, the relationship was as wholesome a hand-holding affair as could be desired by an overprotective mother, worried that her daughter might make the same mistake that she herself had nineteen years earlier.

McCord's mother became a friend and confidant of Wynonna's. Mrs. McCord became something of a surrogate mother—someone Wynonna needed in her life, someone older with whom she didn't additionally have to toe up to the expectations of a business relationship.

Wynonna was so smitten with her first puppy love by the time that the Judds went into the studio with Maher and Potter to finally record "Mama He's Crazy" that she sang her heart out. When she was finished, everyone in the studio noticed the hair on their arms standing on end.

Naomi's fiery, competitive relationship with her oldest

daughter cooled down a few notches in the months following Wynonna's dramatic arrival at Woody Bowles's doorstep. Sometimes it was almost normal. In a way, it was a great relief to Naomi that her daughter was finally out on her own. They were able to work together in the studio, giddy as a pair of pajama-party teens, helped along in part by Ken Stilts's increasingly regimented approach to their daily routine. He figured that busy hands were happy hands, and besides, Wynonna needed his constant reminders to show up for crucial meetings. She still tended to space out into her own world. The Judds had held firm in negotiations with RCA for complete artistic control of their recorded product. They *had* to get along there, because they, Maher, and Potter had agreed to make every creative decision together—not majority rule, but all or nothing. RCA had given them enough rope to either lasso their star or hang themselves.

"I think they knew from the first minute they met us that we wouldn't take any talking to," Naomi said. "I think they sat back and looked at us and saw that we were two crazy redheads [though they were, in fact, natural brunettes at the audition and remained so up until their second RCA album] that you'd better not mess with. RCA just had to turn us loose if they wanted us. We couldn't work any other way."

By the first weeks of 1984 the mini-LP was in the hands of the record pressing plants. Maher had taken the best of the Judds' eclectic repertoire with songs like "John Deere Tractor" and added to it exquisite off-the-wall numbers like "Blue Nun Cafe," Naomi's own "Change of Heart," and, of course, Kenny O'Dell's masterful "Mama He's Crazy." Pegged for the first single was a little-remembered 1975 hit single for Elvis Presley, a song called "For the Heart." When Wynonna Judd got through with the word "you" in the second line of the tune, it had two syllables ("yo-hoo") and was an immediately identifiable trademark of the new duo. The song was retitled for them "Had a Dream (For the Heart)," and in the first months of 1984 it launched the Judds into the Top 20 of *Billboard* magazine's country charts.

Bowles, reverting to the role of publicist, worked with RCA to coordinate a special Nashville debut party for the abbreviated album, titled simply *The Judds: Wynonna and Naomi.* Reporters for Nashville's two daily newspapers, all the entertainment industry trade publications, representatives of every country-music fan magazine that even pretended to publish, and as many free-lance journalists crowded the marvelous hardwood and marble decor of the old Candyland restaurant and soda shop in midtown Nashville for the event.

Candyland had never before been the site of such a media event. It was out of the way for the music business, and finding a place to park in its general vicinity was not easy on a weekday, since it is located in the middle of the downtown financial and shopping district. At the party, each Judd had the same dark brown hair, but they carried themselves quite differently. Naomi was bouncy and vibrant, whereas Wynonna was almost overwhelmed at the crowd in the candy shop. She stood back by the small riser before their brief performance, talking to her handlers and the few close friends who had come to support her while her mother circulated and shook hands.

No one who attended regretted it when Potter and the Judds took a makeshift stage at the back of the room and performed as they would for the next four or five months on a promotional tour of major radio stations. As "Had a Dream" began to climb the charts, Naomi punched her last hospital time clock and Wynonna turned in her final work slip to the temporary agency she'd been working for on and off since graduation. Naomi noted February 1, 1984 as the day on which she "emptied her last bed pan."

Now they began working at their career in earnest, full-time and nonstop. As they took off as an acoustic trio to serenade the outer lobbies of some of the biggest country radio stations in the nation, Woody Bowles and wife Elaine Ganick found to their relief that several days out of the week they had only two babies to contend with for a change: their own twins. Bowles was kept off-balance from living with his client on a twenty-four-hour basis. It was a strain on him and his wife, both of whom had been getting only the limited sleep that infants allow parents in their first twelve months anyway. But the arrangement held. The road was full of surprises and gratifying exchanges with deejays. They were the gigglingly happy mother and daughter of their press releases, women who looked like sisters and sang heart-warming music. No one outside the immediate camp knew about Wynonna's living arrangements. No one but their driver and Potter knew how the physical strains of the road eventually began to tell on the mother-daughter relationship again.

The blitzing schedule was fun for the first few months, especially for Wynonna, who got along with the idea of hotels and maid service just fine. When questioned as to whether she was liking the experience, she would reply, "Yeah, for the last three months I haven't had to clean up my room or nothin'."

"Yesterday she thought she was having a terrible time getting room service; then she realized that we were home," Naomi would say with a laugh.

But for Naomi, it was no easy life as a fifty-fifty business partner with a daughter whose stubborn laziness had nearly driven her to violence a year earlier. Wynonna still hadn't grown up much. In fact, life on the road as a singing star whose fame grew by the day threatened to reinforce that adolescent outlook. There is certainly nothing implicit in road life to make an entertainer become suddenly responsible. That's why artists hire road managers. But the Judds didn't have a road manager at that stage. They had only each other, and Wynonna continued to treat Naomi as "mama the keeper."

"Mama, what room am I in?" one reporter overheard her say at the beginning of one of their early interviews on the road. Things like that became exasperating for Naomi, who also had to worry about whether their sound system was set right at a showcase gig. Stilts had bought them two different matching stage costumes, but Wynonna was forever forgetting to get hers washed, or leaving it at home altogether. Naomi was not the kind of woman to whom little details like punctuality and tidiness were insignificant. Wynonna's blissful ignorance was sending her up the walls, and they began to fight with great frequency once again. Bowles, who had to live with one of them when they were off the road, had to keep a low profile on that account. Ken Stilts was the one who stepped in and asserted a virtually parental control over both Naomi and Wynonna, undercutting Bowles's position in the partnership at the same time.

"Ken gave them a framework," explained Sandy Pinkard. "He gave them a bus and a schedule like something written by Adolf Hitler. Ken was having to get in the middle and moderate and come up with a program whereby they could actually cope together on the road. Ken was really that paternal figure early on. That and his billfold—he was able to hold it together. Woody was just over his head as a player with Ken. This guy has reflexes. It was just a matter of time with those two. If you don't have a pretty big billfold, you aren't going to hold onto an act like the Judds."

Bowles was eventually dealt out of the management company, but with a "golden parachute" and a contractual agreement to simply answer with a smile questions about the inside details of the Judds' business dealings. Wynonna finally did get her own apartment that year, as their second single, "Mama He's Crazy," ran up to top the country charts.

In a brilliant stroke of cross-pollination within the management fold, Pinkard and Bowden had dressed themselves in drag to match the album art to the Judds' mini-album, which also carried "Mama He's Crazy" in its grooves. They sent out posters to match the ones RCA sent out on the Judds. The two of them were often found side by side on the wall in the radio stations that they visited. Looking at the two, you could hardly tell the Dudds from the Judds until you looked closely and realized how funny looking Richard Bowden really is without his glasses. Far from making the Judds laughing stocks, Pinkard and Bowden's humorous recording "Mama She's Lazy" doubled the impact of the song.

"Our airplay pushed that over the top as BMI song of the year," Pinkard said. "We sold as many copies of that as some country artists do on number 1s. The poster thing really did help us a lot. We have been a long time the darlings of morning drive time, but this really increased it, because they were playing those songs back to back. We used the exact same pickers, including Don Potter."

Naomi and Wynonna thought the whole thing was hilarious, showing a very healthy and carefree side that immediately set them off as women with a sense of humor, lacking the petty insecurities that might have gotten Pinkard and Bowden sued by some other acts in the business. Ashley Judd modeled as a Candy Striper in a takeoff on Naomi's nursing background for the Pinkard and Bowden album. The Judds toured with Pinkard and Bowden on several dates during the next year, howling along with the audience when the boys changed into their Dudds costumes and came out to lampoon them. Pinkard reports that they only once took off and left him in a Texas truck stop restroom in his bathrobe at dawn in retribution.

"They took it real good," said Pinkard. "We're real close friends. I've heard them tell that anybody else but us and they would have been horrified."

E·L·E·V·E·N

Growing Pains
Pay Off

Almost before they knew it, Naomi and Wynonna had become stars. Not rich or truly famous, to be sure, but even as Naomi's fellow nurses at Williamson County Hospital flooded the radio stations with calls requesting "Had a Dream," the Judds were becoming two of the most recognizable voices in country music. Flush with the news from the RCA promotion department that their first record was being added to the playlists of dozens of new stations each week, they eagerly made themselves available for interviews and other promotional activities. They were on the way to a syndicated radio show appearance when they first heard their music being broadcast.

"We were going to do an early-morning radio show [for Music Country Network], and [host] Charlie Douglas timed it exactly so we would hear it," Wynonna explained. "When Mama and me got to the studio, we were both red-eyed. It's like your first kiss or your first love: it's something you don't forget."

They had hung around the music business for years, but

never as big-league participants. They were quite green in 1984. Just as Naomi reportedly had to be dissuaded from holding up the RCA negotiations demanding Silver Eagle tour buses and guaranteed plastic surgery if needed to keep her looking like Wynonna's slightly older sister, she had to learn reality on the road from hard experience. At first she wanted to shield her daughter from the difficulties of road life, but Wynonna was far too willing to let her.

"Things just started happening right under my feet, and I just went with it," Wynonna said. She was simply too young and sheltered not to be overwhelmed by what was happening to her. But for the fact that her mother and managers expended considerable energy reminding her to keep her feet on the ground, she might have spun out of control very early in the game.

"To a certain extent I was apprehensive," Naomi confessed. "But not for me. I'm such an adventuress, I'll do anything and I'm not the least bit afraid to try things. I was more apprehensive about her being thrust into show business so forcefully and whether she'd be able to handle it."

Touring for a new act may entail only two or three days a month at first, spinning into two or three days per week if they are lucky. In that regard, the Judds were lucky. Ashley was once again the girl who sat at home and waited. There was pressure from all corners of the family to have her leave Nashville, where her mother simply wasn't available to look after her. She was often lonely, but resisted leaving for the time being.

Success was sweet, but somehow empty at first. When Naomi's success began arriving, she was bereft of the company of many people who had once been close to her. She had split with Larry Strickland around the time of her RCA deal. She could live without a boyfriend and had done so for long stretches of her life.

"She's [a] real ornery, very aggressive, and powerful woman," Wynonna observed. "I mean, she likes to be in control of everything. That's the way she is. I think men look at her as intimidating because she's a businesswoman, and she's smart. I know she acts like 'Oh, I'm Little Miss Homemaker' and all that, but . . ."

Boyfriends would come and go, especially Strickland, but as their records began to climb the charts, she decided that it was time to make peace with her mother. Both women had been too stubborn to open the door of communication between them that had closed in 1977. Polly Rideout had cooled her anger at her daughter over the divorce-trial fiasco, but she had transferred the residual ill feelings from that episode into disapproval of Naomi's life-style and seeming inability to settle down anywhere. With the Judds' record-sales success, Naomi had vindicated her lifelong quest for dreams. The mother and child reunion was long overdue.

Soon after she reconciled with her mother, Naomi returned home triumphant. In the summer of 1984, Ricky Skaggs invited the Judds to perform with him in his own annual hometown charity benefit show in Louisa, Kentucky. Louisa was, coincidentally, where most of Glen Judd's family lived, and where Naomi had spent her childhood summers.

At the same time, Ashland's Paul G. Blazer High School class of '64 was holding their twentieth-year reunion just a few miles away. Naomi took off most of that week to perform with Skaggs, attend her reunion, and generally reestablish herself in an emotional homecoming. Wynonna turned twenty in an atmosphere charged with positives.

The Judds were constantly learning their new trade in an earn-as-you-learn atmosphere. As the pressures on their time and privacy mounted, Naomi soon realized that she couldn't carry Wynonna as a dependent child anymore. Hard as it was to be on both of them, Naomi fought to get her daughter to shoulder at least responsibility for herself while Naomi grappled with tour logistics. Usually, a mother can push a nominally grown-up child out on her own, tell her to "get her act together," and hope it works. But Wynonna *was* part of *Naomi* 's act. Naomi had to live with her daughter's slow maturation process and carry the slack. There was both intense pleasure at sharing the intimacies of this new adventure with each other and a lot of learning to be done by both women in the art of getting along in this new and necessary business relationship.

"It was tough," said Wynonna. "Even though we have eighteen years difference between us, we were both babies in the business. That made us cling to each other for survival. The two of us had to be each other's best friend and be someone to talk to when we had a bad day. We were experiencing some absolutely phenomenal things.

"A lot of people ask what it's like to sing with your mama," she further said. "I tell 'em it depends on what day it is. Monday, it's great. Tuesday, I've done something to make her mad. Wednesday, she's complaining because I was late to the bus. Thursday, we do just fine. Friday, I tell her to go wash a load. I'm not gonna lie about it; mothers and daughters have this love-hate relationship. Your mama can make you the maddest of anybody in your life, but she can give you the most stability and support of anyone."

The initial radio promotional tour during the spring of 1984 took them out with Don Potter, a calming influence who was more than willing to sit back and read his Bible quietly while Naomi and Wynonna bickered and argued with each other. As that first six months saw their second record go to the top of the country charts, they shifted gears and began opening real shows in front of real audiences, ranging from several hundred to nearly ten thousand. They were confident of their music, but no one coached them on stage presence, or even on what they should do between songs. By the autumn of 1984, Potter led a full band for them. Their first really major concert was in Omaha, Nebraska, as opening act for the Statler Brothers.

"It was terrifying," Naomi observed. "Here Wynonna was hardly out of high school and had just quit her job as a secretary and I had just quit mine as a nurse, and all of a sudden I'm standing behind that curtain knowing there are nine thousand people on the other side. As the curtain started up I looked over at Wynonna and thought my throat was gonna close."

According to Naomi, Wynonna turned to her and whined agitatedly, "Mama take me home *now*."

"I thought about it, but the curtain was already up to our knees and we couldn't run," Naomi continued. "Then I thought, 'Wait a minute, this is what we've been working for. This is exactly what we've wanted.' And by the time the curtain was all the way up and we had to step up to the microphones, it was pure enjoyment."

As that first year of adjustment and learning unfolded, both women were having the time of their life being recognized by strangers and having radio personalities rave over their music. But for each moment of glory there were hours of tedious highway travel. When they weren't arguing, they leaned on their zany senses of humor to get them through quick changes in truck-stop bathrooms, sack after sack of fast food, the exquisite boredom of bus life, and the grueling physical demands of being "on" when they were supposed to be.

"I never dreamed the work would be this hard," Wynonna explained. "I think people have this idea that Naomi and Wynonna Judd jet-set all over the world, take bubble baths, and drink champagne, but Mom and I are working really hard. We do up to two shows a day, and we travel to a different state every day."

The thrill of performing and being accepted was enough reward for them at first. Naomi's lust had been for the spotlight rather than for the bankroll. They let Ken Stilts and Woody Bowles handle the financial aspect. Naomi, the more business-minded of the Judds, eventually asked the right questions and found that fun was about all they were likely to accumulate for a while.

"The first year, it's like starting a new business," Naomi explained. "You go so deeply in debt because of the bus, the payroll, the costumes and equipment . . . The first year you are the opening act for everybody else; the second year you have to buy the production set and you have to get the semi.

"You know what I did when I got the first little bit of a check from RCA?" she said. "I got medical insurance and life insurance, and I bought three burial plots. That's real glamorous."

Wynonna, of course, spent her first RCA monies on permanently changing her name.

Traveling together, performing together, called to meetings together when they were back in Nashville—the Judds argued almost daily. Naomi nagged at Wynonna's shortcomings and gave unwanted advice about life, love, and weight control. Sometimes they'd scream at each other late into the night over Wynonna's late arrival backstage or back on the bus after the show, or any number of similar complaints. Wynonna, for her part, stoked the fires with bitter resentment against her mother's oppression.

They fought, but later they'd laugh about it. Called on everywhere they went to give interviews to the media, the confusion of their private and professional lives usually spilled over into their interviews. It was as though the reporter were a combination family counselor-referee-innocent bystander shot by an often hilarious cross fire of words as Naomi and Wynonna competed to tell their side of the story and pull pranks on each other.

"I'm so bitterly honest that when we first started doing interviews and people asked how we got along, I'd say, 'Well, right now I'm real mad at her,' if we'd had a fight that morning over her borrowing my makeup and not returning it or something," Naomi explained to the Huntington *Herald-Dispatch*. "They want us to be perfect, to say that we never fought, but I figured out, 'Hey, it's okay to fight.'"

"I'm a little rebellious at times," Wynonna said. "I know I am. I'm stubborn. There's times when I get real tired of Mom. I don't want to deal with her, to hear her dramatic hillbilly stories, to hear her tell me what to do. And there are times when I actually enjoy being with her.

"Here I am in the music business, and all my girlfriends are going away to college, getting married, moving away from their parents . . . I get kind of angry when I'd rather go to the movies that sit in a meeting for an hour. I didn't want to hear Mom's dramatics," she said.

Understandably, Naomi seemed unable to untangle her mothering instincts from her own rebellion at her irresponsible partner.

"When we first started out performing, I'd plug in her curling iron and iron her dress while I was trying to get myself ready, and I had as much to do as she did," Naomi complained.

In fact, she could kid herself about her rampant mothering instincts spilling over into touring.

"I've been a mama, a housewife, and a homemaker since I was seventeen years old, and I was wondering when I was going to get the urge to get out and mop and wax the freeway," said Naomi. "But, this is the fantasy to beat all fantasies, I'll tell you."

The Judds' wildfire success had started early enough in 1984 and had snowballed so solidly through that year that they were top contenders for several awards to be given at the Country Music Association awards show that October, including vocal group, single of the year, and the Horizon Award. When they walked away with the Horizon Award, they were essentially marked as "best new act." Their appearance fulfilled Naomi's most garish dream of hillbilly extravagance. They dressed in antebellum ball gowns and had their hair dyed electric purple-red. Backstage, they were exuberant, giggling like a couple of school girls. After a brief press conference, Naomi was immediately surrounded by a group of well-wishers, mostly men, while Wynonna wandered off almost unnoticed. With her as she picked over the finger food at the grand buffet tables was Steven McCord.

Woody Bowles was backstage at the Grand Ole Opry House that night to congratulate them—and to hint at the changes that such a rapid accumulation of accolades was likely to cause.

"Woody came to me and said, 'You *do* realize, as of now, your lives, professionally, have changed,' " Wynonna explained. "In other words, we're expected to get up on stage as professionals alongside people like Lee Greenwood who've been performing ten or twenty years, who've had a chance to make mistakes and get their show together. I mean, Mama and I were still learning how to walk on stage and hold the microphone. We're still learning all the little things, and all of a sudden we're put in these incredible situations and were being expected to handle them and carry them off. I was terrified at times."

The momentum and pressure to tighten their show continued after they were selected to appear on the 1985

Grammy Awards show. Their nomination for best new act marked the first time an act from the country-music ranks had been in that list since 1968, when Jeannie C. Riley's defiant "Harper Valley P.T.A." had propelled her upward as a flash-in-the-pan across-the-board hot ticket. They were chosen as presenters for the February 26 Grammy show; then it was suggested that they might also be tapped to perform on the program. Wynonna wisecracked about the stresses that she felt: "To me [it] would be wonderful: that way I'd get to throw up twice instead of once."

They won the Grammy for best country performance by a duo or group with vocal in 1985 for "Mama He's Crazy."

Following by a matter of weeks were the Academy of Country Music (ACM) Awards, the West Coast–based honors whose establishment actually predated those given by the Country Music Association (CMA). In ACM competition that year the Judds continued to pile up the kudos. "Why Not Me" won song of the year, and Naomi and Wynonna were named ACM top vocal duet. They had become everyone's darlings.

Their show from the very first was irrepressible, if not polished. Don Potter was responsible for the music, which was quite on the mark. On stage, Naomi sashayed her petticoats around like a flirtatious clogger. Wynonna had not yet learned to seize center stage with her sneering smile and a shake of her pant leg borrowed from Elvis. Their sincerity made up for the lack of experience and is still, when evident, the most compelling aspect of their presentation. Wynonna wasn't always ready when it was time to go on, but she always went on and sang with that clear voice that is still the strongest in country music.

One might think that the warm glow of acknowledgment and honors would wash away their bickering—and it did when they were collecting the awards themselves. But back in their daily grind, they could not stop fighting. Wynonna just didn't have the maturity to be other than an eighteen-year-old awash in the fun of it all. Naomi overreacted to every act of irresponsibility, which generated immediate hostility from Wynonna, and continual acts of rebellion that kept the bus atmosphere charged about half the time. In a lengthy interview with *Country Music* magazine's Patrick Carr, the Judds gave anecdotal insight into their progress as performers and as quarreling relatives.

"Things started getting better right after we did the first album," said Naomi. "It was rough the first year. I mean there were some big-time scenes on the bus and backstage. Ricky Skaggs can tell you about the time we opened for him at the Denver, Colorado, . . . Durango Music Hall and we were just—"

"I had forgotten my outfit," Wynonna interrupted.

"RCA executives had flown in for the show," Naomi continued. "Denver, Colorado, is a big radio market, a huge radio market, and all the radio station guys from the area and everywhere—oh, it was a heavy, heavy night. Probably the biggest concert that we had had. Our manager flew in from Nashville.

"Wynonna, in her supreme, undisciplined nature—we only had two outfits to our names. We had these leather dresses, which had to be put in the cleaners in Nashville for three weeks because it took so long to clean 'em, and we had this other little two-piece outfit, pants and tops, and the hotel was twenty minutes at least, twenty miles maybe. It was a grasslands venue.

"Our piano player sold our concessions, our bass player was our road manager, I was running lights and sound from the stage—and it's like time to throw on your outfit and hit that stage, man. Wynonna didn't have her clothes. See, you have to understand my situation. I am a very professional person. I have always been—"

"Would you like to go see how she winds out the tooth-paste onto her toothbrush?" Wynonna burst in with a giggling insinuation.

"That's just my nature, you know?" Naomi continued, oblivious to her daughter's attempt to lighten the moment with humor. "Like, when we lived in California I was an executive secretary. I'm a detail person; that's the way my mind thinks. I'm organized; I'm together. Believe me, I've got big-time faults. That's one thing that I've sort of figured out. This is called maturation. And man, we hadda, like, keep me away from her because I'm just going to pull her hair out of her head."

At this revelation, Wynonna began to laugh uncontrollably, like children will do in the backseat of a station wagon on a long trip, just when their mom turns and says "You two cut it out back there." Laughing, she rolled on the motel bed where they had chosen to hold this particular interview.

"I was just hysterical," Naomi explained. "I thought, 'Oh my God, what are we going to do now.' Here I am, I feel like I'm the leader of the group, and it's like a typical mother whose kid is—"

"She couldn't ground me though," Wynonna butted in, still giggling. "I mean, what are you going to do, confine me to my bunk for a week without shows?"

Wynonna had hit the nail painfully on the head. Her mother's greatest frustration was that she no longer had any power over her daughter unless she could make the girl accept discipline through sheer force of will. A war of wills between the two was a long siege.

"Another pressure point was that Ricky Skaggs is Mr. Perfectionist," Naomi continued. "When you work with Ricky—and I have so much respect for him—but when he says you open for him at eight, I mean it's seven fifty-nine and counting and when it hits eight o'clock, bam! that curtain goes up and those house lights go out and they want to hear the guitar chord.

"Dig this—you tell me that God isn't watching over us. Our manager, who had flown in for the show [and] had rented a car to drive to the gig, had in his backseat our two suede dresses from the cleaners in Nashville. I had to wear Reeboks; I didn't have the shoes or the earrings that matched the outfit, but I would have gone out there barefoot."

As 1985 rolled into summer, the number 1 hit singles continued to pile up. They got a chance to return to Ashland in their role of celebrities, and they jumped at it. They had done nearly every charity concert they'd been invited to just to get out in front of crowds since "Mama He's Crazy" propelled them into a full-band touring unit. Naomi and Wynonna promised to play a benefit in Ashland to raise money for King's Daughters' Medical Center. It rained and the attendance was far short of expectations, but the show went on. "This town helped me bury a brother and a dad," Naomi explained.

The Louisville *Courier-Journal* sent out their best features writer and a top-notch photographer to cover the event, resulting in statewide recognition that the home girls had indeed arrived. The reporter and photographer followed them around for a couple of days, giving the whole town an idea of just how important they were becoming. Naomi was clearly reveling in the moment, but Wynonna cried in the circus tent they had for a dressing room because her hair kept falling from the humidity. Naomi, however, took it all in stride. She had gone to her favorite beauty salon in town and held court to old friends, cousins of friends, and complete strangers as the hairdressers got on the phone and told everyone they knew that "Naomi Judd is here—oh, you remember, Diana!" It had been a royal setting for the woman who, as Glen Judd's little daughter, had dreamed fierce fantasies of standing in the spotlight. Her family was amazed at the attention their girls drew.

"I'm still fascinated that they're recognized in public," said Naomi's brother Mark Judd, a Baptist minister in Elizabethtown, Kentucky. "At my graduation from [Louisville's Southern Baptist Theological] seminary . . . after the ceremony and all the graduates marched out, Wynonna was at the door and somebody said, 'Wynonna?' and I thought to myself, 'What a coincidence.' It didn't occur to me that this would be a fan who'd recognized her. It amazed me that my niece would have such fame."

There were get-togethers with most of the family—including in-laws—but a reunion with Daddy Glen would be more difficult. Naomi's father had become very sick. They had seen him since the divorce, but he never asked what they were up to; and though Wynonna sometimes wagged her guitar into the house, he never suggested that he'd like to hear the child play—so she hadn't. The years had not been good to him, nor had he taken particular care of himself. Now he was dying.

Visiting him on his deathbed, Naomi took what comfort she could in the half-hallucinatory professions of affection that poured out of the dying old man. Not long after Glen Judd's death, the demo tape of Jamie O'Hara's tune "Grandpa (Tell Me 'bout the Good Old Days)" was played for them by Brent Maher, who thought they should record it. Naomi broke down in tears for her father on the spot, but wisely chose to keep the song for their next album.

As the country-music industry gathered to honor its own during Nashville's Country Music Week in October, the Judds again earned CMA awards. In 1985 they were elected vocal group of the year, and "Why Not Me" beat out Lee Greenwood's heavily favored Las Vegas–style salute to patriotism, "God Bless the U.S.A.," to earn single-of-the-year honors.

Ashley, who was fifteen when her mother and sister began to tour seriously, finally decided against staying on in Franklin by herself. First she moved to Ashland to live with Polly, then went to live with her father who had returned to Lexington. Naomi suffered pangs of guilt for leaving her youngest daughter.

"I've got a truck-stop relationship with Ashley," she explained. "It's extremely painful for me at certain times."

She missed being able to hug her youngest when she was sad, to offer comfort as she felt a mother should. Ashley would become emotional when an especially intimate interview by her mother and sister was published, or when a song like "Grandpa" caught her in a wistful mood. Naomi recalled one such truck-stop phone call to Ashley.

"She was just sobbing," Naomi explained. "She said, 'Mommy, I just read about you in *McCall's* magazine. I just saw you on "Hour Magazine," and they've been playing your album on the radio. I miss you.' I had to keep myself from jumping on a plane and going right home."

While her mother and sister were away building their careers, Ashley graduated from Sayre School, a quality private academy in Lexington, and started college at a state university. Her mother invited her along on the bus with them one summer, but the younger Judd seemed fated to keep in touch with her family from roadside phone booths and over the radio.

Each consecutive round of music awards shows held another trophy for the Judds' mantel. The Grammy show of 1986 brought them honors again for best country performance by a duo or group with vocal for "Why Not Me." At the ACMs they took the Hat Award as top vocal duet. Their concert performance changed that year in line with the theme of their 1985 awards acceptance speeches, stressing the dream-come-true aspect of their success. They were pretty bowled over by the constant attention and growing adulation and tended to practically preach at their audiences to hold tight to their dreams because, as they said, "if our dreams can come true, you should ask yourself, why not me," typically using that as an introduction to the song by the same name.

The Judds had been paying their dues as an opening act for about two years when their first chance to headline a show came by chance. They had opened shows for Conway Twitty, Kenny Rogers, and the Oak Ridge Boys. They had gone as warm-up for Neil Young on a two-week engagement across Canada, but they had yet to be the headline, which earns the lion's share of the gate receipts. Naomi recalled their first headline show as a fill-in for Merle Haggard, who had simply gotten depressed and taken himself out of the concert schedule without telling anyone else. It happened at the Los Angeles Universal Amphitheatre.

"We flew in Saturday afternoon, and our manager met the plane and said, 'We've got a serious problem. Nobody can find Hag,'" Naomi said. "That was a problem because the show had sold out so fast that the promoter had booked us for a second night and we were without a headliner. We put four phone lines in our hotel room and began calling people. We called Willie Nelson, Hank Jr., and George Jones, and everybody else we could think of; but we couldn't find another act to headline."

Finally, they got Southern Pacific, a reborn-country merger of former Creedence Clearwater Revival and Doobie Brothers musicians with ever-changing lead singers, to open for them. The Judds became the headliners. The promoter offered to refund the price of admission to anyone dissatisfied with the lineup, but the outdoor theater remained full for both performances. The Judds had arrived.

Wynonna's relationship with her mother seemed to develop into one of fewer but angrier fights.

"Sometimes, I just want to say, 'Mom, get your own bus,' " she confessed.

To help her relax on the road, she bought an English rat terrier, named it Loretta Lynn, and began carrying it on the bus as her "cuddle-buddy." She was being affected by the fame and the life-style, so that it was all her mother and manager could do to keep her ego in check.

She was constantly having to be reminded that she was still the same girl who three years earlier had worked as a secretary so that she wouldn't act out in front of their fans. She took their correction to heart, but the conflicting sensations of fame and grinding hard work built up a pressure within her that needed a way to get out. Luckily for her, Don Potter was there with an answer that didn't lead to the drugs or alcohol that so many other touring musicians have turned to from the very same pressures.

"He has been a major blessing in my life," Wynonna said. "I wouldn't [otherwise] have gotten the spiritual awareness I've received."

But Potter was no longer on the road with the band that year. He found touring too demanding. Just as he had previously turned his back on his instrument after deciding that it was mastering him instead of the other way around, he now only visited with Wynonna when she was home and played in the studio when they recorded. His calming presence was gone from the tour bus.

The road continued to tempt and pressure her. During 1986 she combined the outlooks of "praise the Lord" and "where's the party." Her relationship with McCord grew through the inevitable changes, then cooled considerably. She was outgrowing her sweet Franklin boyfriend, at the same time gaining some sense of quiet independence from, perhaps even power over, her mother. She could never exercise authority over her mother, but she found the strength to ignore her mother's meddling advice on life which continued even after the nagging over past irresponsibility declined. Wynonna was still moody, but she was learning not to let her mother get under her skin as much.

It was a vastly more confident Wynonna Judd who stepped in front of the cameras with Naomi to receive the 1986 CMA vocal group award for the second consecutive year. She spoke with self-possession, even as her mother babbled in hyperactive, flabbergasted hillbilly excitement in her third appearance at the podium in as many years. It was apparent to everyone that Wynonna had changed; she was growing up.

In late 1986 a project was proposed that held the potential of reuniting their family—Naomi, Wynonna, and Ashley—in Los Angeles. At Twentieth Century Fox, someone decided that the zany, animated duo would be good for a situation-comedy television series.

"I wanted it to be like the Monkees go to visit Ozzie and Harriet," Wynonna explained.

Naomi refused to even consider the proposition until Stilts told her that Ashley could be in the show if Naomi wanted it that way. The idea was to model the characters and plots as closely to Naomi's life story as possible, sticking to the girls' own personalities as well.

"Ashley and I have a very love-hate relationship," said Wynonna. "She thinks I'm the most overbearing, dramatic sister that ever was, and I think Ashley is totally full of crap. It is really wonderful to sit in the room and watch the three of us go off on one another—and that's exactly what happens."

The family reunion never panned out, though. Somewhere between the floating of the concept at Twentieth Century Fox and the inability of screenwriters to even get the Judds to agree on character names for themselves, the pilot never got filmed. It is possible that someone at Fox finally heeded Naomi's own warning at an early meeting with television executives when she asked, "Has it occurred to any of you guys that we can't act?"

In late 1986 Brent Maher and the Judds picked out songs for their fourth Judds album, *Heartland*. Naomi and Wynonna couldn't resist picking Presley's "Don't Be Cruel" for the lead single from that LP. Naomi had mixed in the gospel music industry in 1979 when she first got to Nashville, which is where she found Strickland, a former member of the Stamps Quartet. The Stamps had been Elvis Presley's third gospel backup vocal section, after the Jordanaires and the Imperials, and Strickland had been a part of the group at that time. His stories of Graceland and Elvis in his latter days fascinated Naomi.

Naomi and Wynonna both eventually developed major obsessions with the late King of Rock 'n' Roll, so much so that they commandeered Graceland for a private tour and joked about Ken Stilts's short, portly resemblance to Presley in his last days. They decided that, after he had given Naomi a diamond ring and a fur coat over two Chistmases, they should buy an Elvis Presley stage costume for their manager.

"You have to understand that we are the man's biggest fans in the universe," Wynonna explained.

"Elvis is the reason my boyfriend and I are together today," Naomi explained. "My boyfriend was bass singer for the Stamps Quartet and lived with Elvis. He had some Elvis clothes from when Elvis was bloating out. Larry is six feet tall and 170 pounds. When they'd be at Graceland, Elvis would take Larry up to his bedroom and give him clothes.

"Larry walked in on me the night "Mama He's Crazy" went number 1. So, I hadn't seen him in a year and a half, and I called him one day to see if he'd sell me an Elvis outfit. I knew I was the only person in the world he'd sell it to. And we got back together after that."

Ironically, the two revisited Presley hits were the only Judds records through their first ten not to reach the number-1 chart position. "Had a Dream" had been a hit single for Presley and appeared on two of his albums, but few people who heard the Judds' Top-20 version remembered the earlier record. This was not the case with "Don't Be Cruel." Although it reached the Top 10 for the Judds early in 1987, it had probably been kept from the top of the charts simply by a backlash from Presley fans who were insulted that anyone would try to replace the King's version of the classic hit.

Naomi's Tennessee nursing license lapsed December 31, 1986, but it seemed unlikely that she'd ever need it again. What little healing she practiced was administered to Wynonna. Allergies and overwork plagued Wynonna on the road, sometimes causing her throat to swell so tight that she could barely breath. Naomi administered her medicine and nursed her through those times, but there were no more bedpans in that woman's future. In the first weeks of 1987, RCA underwrote a tour of England and the Benelux countries, where American country music has fans. Prior to this overseas jaunt, the Judds had only gone as far out of the country as Canada.

The British didn't know what to make of Naomi's theatrically exaggerated Kentucky accent, but their music found favor in every music hall they played. Naomi talked Ken

GROWING PAINS PAY OFF

Stilts into a short vacation for the Judds in Switzerland, their first real time off since early 1984. Stilts proved his financial acumen by arranging for the cover photography for their planned 1987 Christmas album to be shot while they were there, thus transforming the trip into a possible tax write-off. They had reached the point in their careers where the skill of keeping income was required, instead of balancing a constant deficit flow. They at last could skim the cream.

"I do feel that my mom has really worked hard and deserves this," Wynonna explained. "Ever since I was eight years old she's worked two jobs to support us. There are times when I can remember her on the phone begging the landlord to let her send the rent in late.

"In my case, the Cinderella story is kind of true. It was like I woke up one morning and we were successful. But I look at Mom and I see a forty-year-old woman who's starting a brand new career with her kid, who's worked herself to death and who's sacrificed a lot because of Ashley and me. So people say that it happened overnight, but I think if they take a look at Mom and realize that she's been a single parent and really had to struggle and do without, then they'd realize it's been justified."

In 1987 the Judds' continued popularity was marked by receipt of their third consecutive Grammy for best country performance by a group with vocals for "Grandpa," an ACM award as top duet, and their third straight CMA award as vocal group of the year. Naomi said that they hadn't changed much as people: "All of a sudden we're in a goldfish bowl, but I still feel [as if] we are like anybody else." If their personalities hadn't been modified by their success, the way they lived certainly had.

The Judds were brought face to face with the changes in their circumstances over the previous three years when they volunteered as celebrity honorary chairmen for the Middle

Tennessee United Way fundraising campaign in 1987. When the announcement was made, the Judds toured the community center and second-hand clothing store at the Bethlehem Center that were funded by the organization. There they saw sights that reminded them of their own earlier shopping outings. Following a ceremonial luncheon, Naomi, plainly moved, shared her feelings.

"This is a very emotional day for Wynonna and me," Naomi explained. "This is where Wynonna and I bought her school clothes. I saw some very familiar dishes down there . . . As we were eating the chicken à la king and listened to the speeches, it began to hit me."

The Judds' music—the great songs they've recorded and the undeniable chemistry of their blended voices—is the secret of their success. Wynonna's voice has been called the fire, Naomi's the smoke. Wynonna's vocal chords are obviously the more outstanding of the two, but criticism that her mother is simply riding her coattails misses the point.

Naomi's low, nasal harmonies do more than complement her daughter's lead; they often infiltrate Wynonna's vocal pattern almost as though nature had encoded their separate voices to fill the gaps in each other. Naomi's quirky harmony lines, added to the high third part Wynonna often adds over her own melody, create a resonance that registered on Don Potter when all the hair on his arms stood on end the first time that he listened to them sing together.

Great vocal combinations in the annals of country music often come from families. The Everly Brothers, Alton and Rabon Delmore, the Glaser Brothers, the Osborne Brothers, and the Stanley Brothers come to mind as examples. There are no female teams in that list. Country-music record buyers have historically been women interested in men singers. Other than Mother Maybelle's Carter Family, with her daughters and nieces, there are no instances of commercially notable mother-daughter teams in modern country-music history.

Naomi and Wynonna Judd are unique as a country mother-daughter duo. As a viable female country ensemble, they far outstripped the sales of Cheryl and Sharon White, who with father Buck had found a niche as a family vocal group prior to the Judds' emergence. Female vocal groups such as the Forrester Sisters, Sweethearts of the Rodeo (both of whom are sisters acts), and the Girls Next Door owe their opportunities on major labels to the Judds' success, just as all self-contained country and country-rock bands owe their opportunities to Alabama's breakthrough. Similarly, all the individual "stars" of commercial country music of the forties and fifties were in the debt of Roy Acuff, who first stepped out of a string band to claim the recognition of fans.

The Judds' acoustic approach harkens back to the traditional country roots that they claim, along with their other musical influences. Standing true to their mountain soul influences has even resulted in adding a "new" instrument to the Nashville sessions scene. Their music drew dulcimer musician David Schnauffer to Nashville, where he hung around Brent Maher's Creative Workshop studio office until he got a chance to play songs on Judds albums, including "The Sweetest Gift," "Rockin' with the Rhythm," "River Roll On," and "Away in a Manger" on the Christmas album.

"It's led to a lot more session work," said Schnauffer of his Judds affiliation. "As far as I know it was the first time a dulcimer had ever been used on a modern major-label recording project."

Naomi's dreams and her stubborn insistence on following them are an important part of their appeal to their fans. The Judds have been especially appealing to country-music fans because they came from common jobs to sudden star-

dom, instead of having years of honky-tonk nightclub experience or second-banana music to color their perceptions and
reactions. "We're just two redheaded country girls," Naomi
declared once. "Our story is just not normal."

Fans identified with this mother and daughter who came
from amongst them to live out this peculiar version of the
American dream.

"We bucked the system," said Naomi.

Though she is humble in the face of questions about
fame, Naomi Judd was by no means ever an ordinary woman.
She spent the first twenty-five years of her life trying to screw
up the nerve to live out her fantasies; the ten years after that
she existed as an all-American gypsy living the U-Haul odyssey on a quest for a vaguely conceived but strongly believed-
in destiny. She once sized herself up this way: "To be per-
fectly honest, I'm a country girl. I get real crazy. I have
believed all my life that happiness is not at the end of the
road but all along the way. I believe in celebrating life. I love
to smell the roses. That's the way I am."

Her travels and life-style experiments and her dabblings
in modeling and the film industry were pieces of the puzzle,
but the key was her rediscovery of Kentucky. It was on her
return there that she put the final touches on the aesthetic
and system of values that would later define the Judds' image
and music. It was up on Bighill that her eldest daughter first
opened her throat to the voice that would, as had her mother's youthful beauty, dictate the contours of her life before
she herself could reach adulthood. It coincidentally provided
the engine to drive Naomi's great American dream machine.

Wynonna is young. It will be years before she needs a
surgical tuck here to shore up a timely sag, or collagen injec-
tions there to fill in the wrinkles. She grows more confident
with every performance, with every recording session. As
Naomi put it once, "[Wynonna] hasn't had her heart broke

yet." Naomi, who knows the costs of making dreams come true as late in life as have her own, is secretly not so secure.

"I wake up everyday praying it's not a dream," she said. "When I'm home, I keep those awards sitting on the table at my bedside. I reach over and touch them to make sure they are real."

T·W·E·L·V·E

The Stories Behind the Hits.

Buddy Killen, owner of the largest Nashville-owned country-music publishing house, Tree International, said, "I don't care if an act has the greatest singing voices in the world. If they don't have a great song to sing, they are not going to have a hit."

The motto of the Nashville Songwriters Association International, "It all begins with a song," reflects the realization by this musical community that the writers lay the foundation upon which all careers are built. Nashville is a songwriter's town, more so than any other major recording capital in America, and the Judds have had first access to the work of some of the greatest country-music songwriters working today, many of whom have tailored their writing especially to suit the Judds' sound and aesthetic.

"Brent, Wynonna, and I listen to everything personally," Naomi explained. "People hand us stuff on the bus when we're pullin' out of town. There's times on the bus when I'm real tired. I've got the back room, and I sort of recluse. And we've got tape decks back there. There are times when I really need sleep, and I just want to sit there and blank out—watch America roll by. But I listen to these songs, because I figure if some songwriter puts his blood, sweat, and tears into a song, the least I can do is give it a real serious ear.

"But what's happened is that the people in Nashville, they've been out to our farm, they know us personally, and they know what we like. They know what we stand for. Nine times out of ten, we go with them.

"What we look for are positive lyrics. Wynonna and I try to stress the positive, upbeat side of life. Of course, it has to have that 'hook' melody, where you come away humming the tune, and of course the vocal harmony parts. If we find a song that somehow stirs up old memories or sets fire to our imaginations, it becomes ours."

Songwriters rarely get the recognition they deserve for their contributions to artists' fame. Their work is done far from the spotlights, often in the cramped writing rooms of Nashville's Tinpan Valley, following up on an inspiration that may have struck someone at any number of odd times and places. Music composition has become more of a business activity than it probably was in the past, when the top songwriters like Mel Tillis, Roger Miller, Harlan Howard, Hank Cochran, or Willie Nelson scribbled lyrics on soiled paper napkins in back-room booths at Tootsie's Orchid Lounge, or rode around the country in rickety tour buses raising hell all night. Nashville has in many ways grown up.

Nevertheless, those unpredictable magic moments when great tunes come together are just as special as they ever were. It seemed appropriate to end with a look behind the scenes at the creative moments that led to many favorite Judd hits. Each song and each writer has a story.

from the mini-LP *The Judds*
"Had a Dream (For the Heart)" (RCA/Curb JK-13673)

writer: Dennis Linde
first entered charts December 17, 1983
peaked at number 17 March 10, 1984

An uproar occurred over the Judds' remake of Elvis Presley's "Don't Be Cruel" in 1987, which was surprising in light of the fact that their first single was also an old Presley record redone. The Judds' first single, "Had a Dream," was written originally for Elvis Presley by Dennis Linde. Presley's version, titled "For the Heart," was issued by RCA in 1975 on the album, *From Elvis Presley Boulevard, Memphis, Tennessee.* It was subsequently included on *Elvis' Golden Records Volume 5* and on the posthumously packaged *Elvis Medley.*

The songwriter, Linde, was born in 1943 in Texas. He began his musical career playing a seventeen-dollar Stella guitar when he was sixteen: "I practiced about four hours a day. It made my hands so sore I had to quit eating with my hands."

He came to Nashville to write songs for Combine Music in 1968 and in 1970 scored his first big songwriting success with a Roger Miller hit, "Tom Green County Fair." Elvis Presley garnered more than 1 million airplays on Linde's "Burning Love" in 1972. Other country hits from Linde's pen are "The Love She Found in Me," as recorded by Gary Morris in 1981, and Don Williams's "Walkin' a Broken Heart" in 1983. He has earned six country and two pop achievement citations, and a Million Airs Award from BMI.

"Mama He's Crazy" (RCA/Curb JK-13772)
writer: Kenny O'Dell
first entered charts April 28, 1984
peaked at number 1 August 4, 1984

About "Mama He's Crazy" O'Dell recalled: "I'm not one of the most prolific writers in the world, but I work all the time. I got the idea for that song off of a soap opera. It was called 'Texas'; pretty much a takeoff on the 'Dallas' thing. As I started to develop the tune, I did it pretty much for them. At the time I was trying to help Naomi get her songs together as a songwriter."

Prior to this song, O'Dell was best known in the country field for writing Charlie Rich's Grammy-, Academy of Country Music-, and double Country Music Association Award–winning platinum hit "Behind Closed Doors." O'Dell also wrote the sixties pop hit "Next Plane to London" for a group called Rose Garden. His "(You Just Gotta Be One of the Most) Beautiful People" marked his debut as a pop artist in the sixties, engineered by a young Brent Maher. He also recorded as a country artist in the seventies.

"Mama He's Crazy" is the most honored Judds record to date, winning for O'Dell Song of the Year and Songwriter of the Year Awards from the Nashville Songwriters Association International (NSAI) and BMI's Burton Award as most performed country composition for 1985. It won a Grammy Award as best country song and was nominated as song of the year in the CMA awards competition. (This song is the only one in the Judds' catalog to appear on two albums, *The Judds: Wynonna and Naomi* and *Why Not Me.)*

"Change of Heart"
writer: Naomi Judd

Although never released as a single, "Change of Heart" introduced the songwriter side of Naomi. " 'Change of Heart' is autobiographical," she explained. "I was madly in love with Larry Strickland, who was Elvis Presley's backup singer, and he broke my heart. I stayed up three days and three nights, couldn't eat or sleep, and I wrote 'Change of Heart.' The song just came out from beginning to end."

from the album *Why Not Me*
"Why Not Me" (RCA/Curb JK-13923)
writers: Harlan Howard, Sonny Throckmorton, and Brent Maher
first entered charts October 6, 1984
peaked at number 1 December 22, 1984

Harlan Howard is the dean of Nashville songwriters, having been writing classic country songs since his first tune was recorded when he was only fourteen. Among the well-known tunes that he has written or co-written are "Busted," "The Blizzard," "Heartaches by the Number," "I Fall to Pieces," "I've Got a Tiger by the Tail," "Streets of Baltimore," "Somebody Should Leave," "The Chokin' Kind," and "I Don't Remember Loving You," to name a few that won awards. He is so well known and respected in Nashville that the whole songwriting community holds a party in the BMI parking lot each summer to honor his birthday and raise money for songwriting causes. He was inducted into the NSAI Hall of Fame in 1973.

Maher is the Judds' producer and is noted for his prodigious ability to add a little seasoning to a song and boost its overall appeal—"copping the groove" in songwriting parlance. Sonny Throckmorton's credits include "Middle Age Crazy," "Last Cheater's Waltz," "I Wish You Could Have Turned My Head (And Left My Heart Alone)," "If We're Not Back in Love by Monday," "It's a Cheatin' Situation," "Waiting for the Sun to Shine," and "The Cowboy Rides Away." He has to his credit fifteen number-1 records. He has been named songwriter of the year four times by various music trade magazines and has twice been named songwriter of the year (in 1978 and 1979) by NSAI and was then inducted into the NSAI Hall of Fame in 1987.

"Why Not Me" originated with a Sonny Throckmorton melody. About writing the song, he recalled: "I had the melody, and I had been singing it for maybe three or four years. Never could really get something to go with it. I'd sing something like 'How 'bout me,' but it wasn't happening, so I just hung onto it. I hadn't been writing with anybody at that time, and Harlan had just woke up from about seven years off and decided he wanted to write again, so he called me. I hadn't ever written with Harlan before, but I wasn't gonna let that one pass up.

"One Sunday morning he woke me up and said today's the day, come over. Brent Maher showed up, and I hadn't really met him before either. I think maybe we wrote three songs that morning. That lick on the guitar on 'Why Not Me,' which is as big a factor as anything in making that song a hit, I believe that Brent Maher come up with that lick after he had taken the song and left our little excursion that morning."

"Girls Night Out" (RCA/Curb JK-13991)
writers: Brent Maher and J. H. Bullock
first entered charts February 2, 1985
peaked at number 1 April 27, 1985

Jeffery Hawthorne Bullock is an ASCAP-affiliated writer who lives in Antlers, Oklahoma.

"Girls Night Out" was crafted to meet the Judds' specific needs. Once again, Maher's knowledge of his production clients' performance strengths and personal preferences provided a custom fit. It became something of an anthem for their 1986 tour.

"Love Is Alive" (RCA/Curb JK-14093)
writer: Kent M. Robbins

first entered charts June 8, 1985
peaked at number 1 August 31, 1985

Robbins, a Kentuckian and a former English major at
Vanderbilt University, has found Charley Pride his most pro-
ductive source of number-1 records. While Robbins wrote for
Pride's publishing company, the singer topped the charts
with "When I Stop Leavin' (I'll Be Gone)," "You're My Ja-
maica," and "I Don't Think She's in Love Anymore." He has
had five number 1's, including this hit by the Judds, and
additionally has written Top Ten tunes for John Anderson
("She Just Started Liking Cheating Songs") and Dottsy's only
major hit, "(After Sweet Memories) Play Born to Lose
Again."

"Mr. Pain"
writers: Naomi Judd and Kent M. Robbins

This is the second Naomi Judd–written tune ever released. Like the first, it remains an album cut. " 'Mr. Pain' I
wrote after one of my girlfriends got her heart stomped on
real hard by a guy," Naomi said. "I really want to write more
songs. I'm about to bust with song ideas. I've seen so much on
the road . . ."

from the album *Rockin' with the Rhythm*
(This album, by the way, was originally scheduled to come
  out under the title *Give a Little Love.*)
"Have Mercy" (RCA/Curb JK-14193)
writer: Paul Kennerley
first entered charts October 5, 1985
peaked at number 1 December 22, 1986 (stayed number
  1 for two consecutive weeks)

Kennerley is a tall, handsome Englishman whose fascination with the American South and country music led him

to compose his first two works. A pair of artistically important concept albums called *White Mansions* and *The Legend of Jesse James* featured between them such musicians and singers as Johnny Cash, Waylon Jennings, Jessi Colter, Charlie Daniels, Levon Helm, Albert Lee, Rosanne Cash, Emmylou Harris, Eric Clapton, and Rodney Crowell.

He moved to Nashville with Emmylou Harris in the mid-1980s, and the two married soon thereafter. Kennerley is largely responsible for Harris's brilliant but commercially unsuccessful 1985 concept album *Sally Rose* that paralleled her own early career with country-rock pioneer and legendary rock 'n' roll overdose victim Gram Parsons. Kennerley's British pop sensibilities were apparently aroused to give the Judds an interesting change of pace with "Have Mercy."

"Grandpa (Tell Me 'bout the Good Ole Days)" (RCA/CURB JK-14290)
writer: Jamie O'Hara
first entered the charts February 15, 1986
peaked at number 1 May 10, 1986

Jamie O'Hara is half of the new back-to-basics duo the O'Kanes. He wrote "Grandpa" for himself, but the Judds recorded it just a week later. Writing it was as emotional an experience for him as its appearance so close to Naomi's father's death made it for her.

"The only thing that I can say about it is that I think many songs are therapeutic in some way," O'Hara explained. "I never really knew any of my grandparents. They had all died before I was born. Some songs come from creative experience and from things that songwriters have, and some things come to kind of fill up the holes in some way. . . . They come from something you feel you lack rather than what you have.

"To me a song that manages to reach out and touch people in a certain manner, to me songs like that are gifts. The writer just happens to be at the right time in the right place, and it comes like a gift. It was my turn to receive a nice little gift, and 'Grandpa' was it."

"Rockin' with the Rhythm of the Rain"
writers: Don Schlitz and Brent Maher
first entered the charts May 24, 1986
peaked at number 1 August 9, 1986

As with "Why Not Me," this Judds hit came in a case of beginners' luck, as a pair of talented songwriters who had never worked together cranked out a fabulous new tune on their first date, as it were. Of course, Schlitz had previously penned one of the biggest money-making songs in recent country-music history, "The Gambler," for which he won nearly every award available, including CMA and Grammy honors, but who's quibbling?

"That was the first time we ever wrote together," said Schlitz of his collaboration with Brent Maher on this song. "We went in with no title and no ideas and just sat down and started playing and singing; playing guitars, trying to play a groove. Somehow we got the title; we liked the alliteration. Brent's a great person to write with. He will just lock onto a groove. You know how the chorus overlays, words that weave in and out? We had been talking about European pop and how sometimes they had two lyrics and two melodies that weave in and out over the chord structure. And that's what we did on the chorus. It was a bit of an experiment that worked. Brent told me that day he knew that was a number-1 song."

Schlitz is the only songwriter to have won three CMA Song of the Year awards for three different songs. These came in 1979 for "The Gambler" and in 1986 and 1987 for "On the Other Hand" and "Forever and Ever Amen," respectively, both of which he co-wrote with Paul Overstreet. Notches on his pencil as writer or co-writer also include "40 Hour Week," "Give Me Wings," "Midnight Girl/Sunset Town," "Stand a Little Rain," and "You Again."

"Cry Myself to Sleep" (RCA/CURB JK-5000)
writer: Paul Kennerley
first entered charts October 18, 1986
peaked at number 1 January 24, 1987

"Paul Kennerley has a real unique style of songwriting: very English, very off-the-wall. This song sounded so haunting and mysterious when I first heard it," said Wynonna.

Aside from their cover versions of old standards, this appears to be the only Judds hit single that was originally penned for another artist. Kennerley's wife, Emmylou Harris, was the first to consider recording "Cry Myself to Sleep." When she decided against it, she personally carried the tune over to the Judds and played it for them.

from the album *Heartland*
"Don't Be Cruel" (RCA/CURB JK-5094)
writers: Otis Blackwell and Elvis Presley
first entered charts February 14, 1987
peaked at number 10 April 11, 1987

Presley's name was appended to this song by insistence of Col. Tom Parker, looking out for his boy's interest (and subsequently his own). Otis Blackwell wrote this tune. Blackwell was a talented black suit presser working in a New York laundry who got ripped off, though the people who continue to this day to do such things in the business have a saying:

Half of something is better than all of nothing. Presumably, this is supposed to make the victim of song theft grateful.

Blackwell himself is philosophical about the whole thing: "I was just sitting around and writing [in the midfifties]," he told Joe Edwards of the Associated Press. "The idea just came. It was one of seven I sold to a publisher to get money that week."

Blackwell's additional songwriting legacy contains such timeless classics as "Fever," as recorded by Peggy Lee (for reasons of his own he sold part of the song, which now bears his father-in-law's name as author), and the Jerry Lee Lewis signature "Great Balls of Fire." Incidentally, the only thing the Judds' version and Presley's version really have in common is the use of the Jordanaires as backup vocal group. Of all the Judds' hits, this one had the shortest chart life, going off the playlist after only thirteen weeks, roughly the time it took most of their songs to reach the number-1 position.

"I Know Where I'm Going"
writers: Don Schlitz, Craig Bickhardt, and Brent Maher
first entered the charts May 9, 1987
peaked at number 1 July 18, 1987

Craig Bickhardt has joined fellow singer-songwriters Thom Schuyler and Fred Knoblock in an MTM Records trio, SKB. He took part in an interesting noncontact collaboration between Schlitz and Maher and himself about which Schlitz recalled, "I went on a two- or three-month road trip, driving across the country, staying away from telephones, and when I got back I found I had a record out by the Judds and I'd co-written it with this guy I'd never met before named Craig Bickhardt."

Bickhardt said, "The song began with Brent. He had written that first little guitar lick and he gave a tape of that lick to Schlitz. Schlitz rode around with that lick on a cassette in his car for months, and eventually they wrote an entire song and played it for the Judds. They loved most of it, but when they got to the bridge it left them flat. Brent and Don had discussed the concept and wanted a sort of good feeling, we're-all-going-to-heaven, "People Get Ready" type of song. Brent and I sat down and I started toying around with a new bridge around September of 1986. We finished that song in about an hour, though from conception to finish took several months. This is one of those rare songs where different people are responsible for different parts of the song."

Bickhardt not only wound up helping to write three songs on *Heartland;* Maher also invited him to be one of two rhythm guitars in sessions for the album.

"Maybe Your Baby's Got the Blues" RCA/CURB JK-5255
writers: Troy Seals and Graham Lyle
first entered charts August 22, 1987
peaked at number 1 November 14, 1987

" 'Maybe Your Baby's Got the Blues' is one of my favorites," said Naomi. "Troy Seals, who was chosen songwriter of the year [by a trade magazine], and Graham Lyle, a very unlikely guy from England who wrote 'What's Love Got to Do with It' for Tina Turner—they came by the studio one afternoon and sat on the couch and played us that song. And I just went bonkers [and] said, 'Good God, this is the women's national anthem.' "

The Judds' music has earned gold and platinum records from sales exceeding five hundred thousand and one million albums, and there seems no end to such performance in the foreseeable future. It is rare for such vocal talent as Wynonna Judd's to be matched with such sympathetic harmonies as those quirky complementary notes of Naomi's. Even rarer is an act that knows who they are. They're successfully bringing their espoused values, dreams, and selves into focus with their music without actually tracing their personal histories in the lyrics as other singers have. But then, it would take a country-rock opera, perhaps soap opera, to even approach telling these women's stories in song. For now we'll have to settle for the dreams.

About the Author

Bob Millard is the Nashville correspondent for *Variety*. He is the author of *Amy Grant* and a contributor to the *Country Music Book*.